M000266198

UNCHAIN
My Legacy

HOW OWNING OUR CHOICES
FREES US AND THOSE WE LOVE

AUDRA R. UPCHURCH
FOREWORD BY DERAN YOUNG, LCSW

Unchain My Legacy: How Owning Our Choices Free Us and Those We Love

www.AudraUpchurch.com

Cover and Interior Design | Editing
DHBonner Virtual Solutions, LLC
www.dhbonner.net

ISBN: 978-1-7323003-0-9

Printed in the USA

Dedications

I am dedicating this chapter to my oldest sister Alfreda Evans. I am so thankful for the time to get to know each other; I deeply miss you. **~Sabra Starnes**

To every mom who waits for everyone to go to sleep before she cries, your happily ever after is waiting for you. **~Maya Lynn**

Dedicated to my daughters. Over time you have taught me that hiding only makes it worse. No more hiding, it's time to heal. We are moving as a unit of strength, and I am proud to be leading the way to building a legacy. **~Michele Mikki Jones**

This chapter is dedicated to two very important women who are no longer with me. Nancy J. Fleming and Jacqueline Speller. May you rest in peace. **~Patrice Trice Brown**

This chapter is dedicated to my children whose unconditional love motivates me to become my best self. **~Ann M. Dillard**

This chapter is dedicated to Carlos, my husband of 21 years. He is my biggest fan and cheerleader. He never gives up on me; he's always patient and always kind. He loves me through times when I feel unlovable. Thank you for always supporting me. Love always. **~Tonya Renada Moore**

I dedicate my contribution of this book to my legacy, Kiah, Donovan, and Christopher. Because it was my desire for you to have a brighter future, I stepped out of the shadows of my past. I love you! **~Veda H. Green**

"Unchain My Legacy" is dedicated to the men and women looking to break the cycle of unhealthy relationships, my parents (Debra and Michael), my siblings, and my best friend, Alexus Woods. **~Davina Jennile**

I would like to dedicate this chapter to my greatest love, my son Jhazz. Without you, there is no me. I would like to thank the visionary author Audra R. Upchurch for this opportunity and her belief in me. You believe in me when I do not believe in myself. Thank you. **~Sandra De Greene**

Dedicated to my loving and supportive husband, Emmanuel and my legacy. The children I will raise and/or serve and those who care for them. **~Illiona Illy Okereke**

This book is dedicated to my siblings, Fonda Wilson, Wylinda Williams, and Kermit Wilson Jr. Although the cards life dealt, were unfavorable and heavily stacked against us: abandoned by a drug-addicted father, raised by a mother who never finished college, living in a housing project that fostered a poverty mentality, and eventually placed in the Foster Care system, our legacy was destined to be chained.

But God, by His grace, had another plan. The legacy we are now building is so much more than we could have ever imagined or hoped for. We are a remarkable example that one can overcome adversity through prayer, hard work, and perseverance... That one can unchain their legacy! **~Tearanie Wilson-Parker**

This chapter is dedicated to my family; I love you all. To my husband, Dareece, thank you for being patient with me as I continue on this journey of personal development and for loving me unconditionally. And, to my sons Dominic and Dallas... Mommy loves you. **~Janika N. Joyner**

"I'm so glad they prayed for me
My [grand]mother prayed for me, had me on her mind
She took the time and prayed for me
I'm so glad she prayed."

...excerpt from "Somebody Prayed for Me."
by Dorothy Norwood

Table of Contents

Foreword

*"We cannot wish old feelings away nor do spiritual exercises
for overcoming them until we have woven a healing
story that transforms our previous life's experience and
gives meaning to whatever pain we have endured."*
~ Joan Borysenko

Most therapists will often use the phrase "Secrets keep you sick." Well, if that's true, a lot of black folks are deathly ill! We often carry generations of burdens; so heavy that we are buried under the weight of it.

It takes a very strong person to heal and face the darkness which lies within. It takes an even stronger person to have a conversation with others about the most intimate experiences that have shaped their life. So many of us come from dysfunctional families, and the rule of thumb is that what happens in this house STAYS in this house.

Unfortunately, 99% of people obediently subscribe to that mentality; sworn to secrecy, no matter the cost. Too often, we fear the controversy, our emotional safety, and comfort being wrapped around unhealthy and counterproductive habits that have now spread like wildfire.

If your only tool is a hammer,
you will see every problem as a nail.
— Gambian proverb

When you show the moon to a child,
it sees only your finger.
— Zambian proverb

My first time sharing my story in black and white was in **Unchain Me Mama!** While I wrote, there were moments of shame, fear, and even feelings of disloyalty. I often hear feedback that it was very graphic, brutal, and transparent.

I wanted to be free, I wanted to free others, and I knew that my legacy was waiting to be freed. I longed to be released from the labels and enslavement of those painful experiences... ready to grow and evolve into my full potential.

However, in order to prepare for my future, I needed to understand my past and how it has the tendency to show up each and every day. Not just in my own life, but also in my son's life and in the life of every other soul that I connect with.

Birds sing not because they have answers
but because they have songs.
— African proverb

At the time of this writing, I am a single woman.

A single mother.

NO!

A single BLACK mother!

Some days, this feels like the best gift in the world, and on other days I'm convinced it's a curse. This is a feeling that almost kept me in an unhappy marriage... one that keeps many women in even worst situations; for some, even to the point of death. The shame and stigma associated with being a single black mother can be enough to question if you have a legacy at all.

Therefore, many of us overcompensate by spoiling our children rotten or rejecting them because they remind us of too many un-kept promises. I'm not sure which one of these is worse, yet I do know that women are a vital source of life.

Not just biological mothers, but all those who pour into the youth of their communities and graciously share wisdom on matters of the heart. This gift of femininity that we hold allows us to care for others; deeply, unconditionally, and at times, sacrificially.

We are the undervalued planters and waterers of life. Nevertheless, we do it so that future generations may grow from both our pain *and* our beauty.

We desire to bequeath two things to our children;
the first one is roots, the other one is wings.
— Sudanese proverb

After writing my first chapter, I now know that the story has only just begun. I'm free to write a new one each day; one that builds upon a strong foundation of courage, acceptance, self-compassion, and forgiveness. The very best gift I can give the future is to truly love myself today!

It is my hope that this book inspires you to trust love, be vulnerable, and to unchain the powerful legacy that may be hidden deep inside your wounded heart.

Get in touch with your own story as you travel this unique path toward the discovery of what it means to truly be free...

To unchain your legacy!

Deran Young, LCSW
Founder of ***Black Therapists Rock***
www.blacktherapistsrock.com

Acknowledgments

As we were compiling this book, I found my father;
who I never knew. It took 48 years for me to see the face of the
man whom I look so much like. So, I dedicate this book to
the late Fred Douglas Perry-Winston.

My father.
My daddy.
I never knew you.
But I still love you.
Sleep in peace...

Your daughter,
Audra

Introduction

AUDRA R. UPCHURCH

My Grandmother died in 2016... and I wasn't sad.

I know that sounds kind of harsh, considering she's my grandmother; but, it's the truth. Since then, I've taken a lot of time to think about why I wasn't as upset as many of my other relatives, and the truth hit me like a ton of bricks.

The first time I told my grandmother that I didn't like her, I was only four, and my mother had left me with her, while she went to look for an apartment. I couldn't understand why she took my sisters and not me, so I was one mad four-year-old. Nana tried to console me as best she could as I repeatedly reminded her that I didn't like her.

Eventually, she stopped talking and began cooking. I sat in the kitchen chair, with my arms folded across my chest, and my little feet swinging back and forth; pouting and attempting to punish her with each tear that rolled down my face. Still, Nana kept cooking and singing her spirituals, as if she didn't have a care in the world. This, of course, made me cry even harder.

Then, she sat a bowl of warm, homemade applesauce, with a few saltine crackers in front of me. One taste and it was all over! I looked up at my grandmother, and said quite matter-of-factly, *"I like you, Nana!"* She let out such a big laugh, that if I close my eyes, I can almost hear her.

That was Nana's favorite story of me. Every time I saw her, she would recite the entire story; again and again.

Did I know that Nana loved me? Sometimes, I did. Other times, it wasn't that apparent.

And, when I think about being homeless as a teenager, she really did nothing to protect me. So, over the years I had become resentful of all of that. I just accepted that maybe, to her, I wasn't as important as some of her other grandchildren that it appeared she was always there for. Towards me, she seemed cold and distant. Therefore, since I wasn't important to her, she would not be important to me or hold a special place in my heart.

As time went on, I convinced myself that I was okay with that.

After her death, I went on a quest to gain a better grasp of who she was, and to my surprise, I discovered that I'm not much different than Nana. You know, often I've been told that I'm cold and that I can be distant... and even downright harsh at times. While I recognize that some of this may be true, in order for me to fully own it, I had to uncover where it came from. Moreover, in doing that, it brought me to not only owning my choices and standing in my truth, but also to a place of greater clarity and appreciation of my grandmother and the interconnection of our legacy.

In 2017, I held my first women's conference, and I was really excited that my daughter was able to attend. Our social media correspondent for the event interviewed my daughter on Facebook Live while I was busy hosting. A few days after the conference, I was catching up on all the live broadcasts, and I was stopped dead in my tracks as I listened to my daughter's interview.

My daughter said, *"When my mother said 'yes' to me, it allowed me to say 'yes' to myself."*

Hearing those words had such an impact on me. It is truly why I'm so passionate about this particular book collaboration and all the stories you're about to read. Many times, we forget that the things we say, and the things we do, have such profound effects on our children. More importantly, if they affect our children, they will affect our children's children, and so on.

As mothers, it's so important that we acknowledge our crap; without shying away from it so that our kids are able to have the emotional freedom to then process it, as they move forward in their own journey. But, when we don't own it, and instead, riddle our response with excuses, we tell our children that what they've been through does not matter. It tells them that they're not important and their experiences don't count.

In essence, we're saying "no" to them.

No, you are not important. *No*, you do not matter. I know you're hurting, *but*.

We have to really be aware of the generational impact it has on them. After looking honestly at myself and how I had such strong similarities to my grandmother, I decided to take a closer look at my family history to piece together where it all came from. Why was it so easy for me to be cold and distant, even to my own child?

I had to take a hard look at the woman I was, in order for me to become the woman I was meant to be; being willing to accept my flaws and all, and most importantly, to stand in the choices I had made that negatively impacted my daughter, if I ever wanted the disconnect in my family to stop with me.

So, as I recounted my family history, my homelessness as a teenager, my tragic experiences of loss and how they significantly affected my daughter, I couldn't help but to take a look at my mom and make the connection with the expression of love that I didn't get from her in my teen years.

My mom suffered from polio at the age of two in the 1940s, and it was really a traumatic experience due to how they dealt with contagious diseases in that era. She was kept isolated in a room by herself for two to three months.

My grandparents would only be able to watch my mother through a glass window; my grandfather crying and broken up that he couldn't hold, touch, or console her. Standing right next to him would be my grandmother... with dry eyes.

Can you imagine being locked in a room and your parents can't touch you, hold you, or console you? They're not there to bandage your knee when you fall, and you can't feel their breath on your face when they hug you? Your only human interaction is with the starchily-clad, masked, nurses and doctors who come in and out of your room; all without the slightest display of affection for you. I can't even fathom the level of emotional and mental devastation that could be, nor how lasting the trauma.

Well, that was my mom's story.

You know, I began to wonder what that must have been like for Nana. What would cause a mother to not respond to her baby girl? The legacy of maternal disconnect in my family is real.

I then learned that my grandmother had been abandoned by the age of two when her mother died. Her father decided that it was too much to raise four children by himself, so he placed his children with various people, and left; never to return.

Separated, they were raised by different families.

Nana was the youngest of the four children, and her life was full of struggle growing up without her siblings. The family that raised her gave her a place to live, and that's all. She lived a life that lacked love, attention or nurturing. Although she married my grandfather, and they had five girls, how would she know how to love and nurture them?

It's hard to give what you've never had.

Do you see how the cycle has gone on and on and on? My grandmother never received love from her mother, because her mother had died, and my mother never received the affection she needed from her mother; and now me... having not received the emotional nurturing I needed from my mother due to her illness, was fated to not give my daughter the love and affection she needed from me, because I was also broken.

It's so easy to excuse our own behavior with our children while condemning our parents and grandparents for theirs. Our lack of forgiveness can impact our legacy for years. But as mothers, if we own our choices, regardless of the circumstances, with no 'ifs,' 'ands,' 'buts,' or 'excuses,' can you imagine how liberating that would be for all of our children?

I'm committed to the buck stopping with me.

So, I decided to *own my stuff*; not blaming my failings on past experiences but identifying where it all comes from so that it doesn't continue.

In owning it, I was able to open my mouth to my baby girl and say, "Honey, I apologize. Do you forgive me for not being there when you needed me to be? Do you forgive me for not hearing you when you were calling out to me? Do you forgive me for not holding you tight enough when I should have? Do you forgive me for not being the mother that I should've been to the amazing gift that God blessed me with; which was you?"

The power of your legacy rests with you.

Will you release the chains?

My grandmother died in 2016... and today, I am sad. Sad, because I understand her so much better now; however, I am also grateful that I have been given an opportunity to own my choices and to facilitate a legacy of freedom.

I love you, Nana.

I Wish I'd Known This When I was 13

ANN M. DILLARD

I can still see the image of myself on that warm summer day. At only thirteen, I stood bent over the large tank of water, which was completely covered with wire, except for the small open section to access water.

Earlier that day I had announced, *"I'll just kill myself."*

Standing there, in the middle of our yard, I contemplated whether or not to jump in. I can still hear voices in the distance saying, *Go ahead.*

Born and raised on the Caribbean island of Jamaica, a rich blend of African and British culture still drenched with the residue of slavery, the lens through which I was raised, taught, disciplined, and learned to interpret the world had already been formed. However, I am not sure which area of this cultural mix impacted my childhood most. Was it the staunch charismatic Christian upbringing or the influence of proper British behavior?

Maybe it was the result of slavery.

Either way, I was raised in a society where feelings were not welcomed and "I love you's" were never expressed verbally.

I remember being exceptionally curious as a child; accused of being inquisitive and talking too much. Neither of which was a good thing in my culture. Therefore, growing up, I never learned how to appropriately express my feelings or emotions. Especially when reasoning with or questioning an adult was a big NO! NO! Children were to be seen and not heard, to speak only when spoken to, and to answer when called. So, at an early age, I discovered that food was a great companion.

I ate when I was excited. I ate when I was sad. I ate when I did not feel like I belonged; which was quite often. There was an incident when my mother sent me to the bakery to purchase two loaves of bread. I bought the freshly baked hard dough bread, and traveling home, I pinched and ate the warm, wonderful smelling bread, bite after bite. By the time I arrived home, only the shells of both loaves were left in the bag. The shame, embarrassment, and consequences were unbearable.

My eating challenges were easily missed because my life was filled with physical activity. It was not until I came to America when I was almost fourteen that my overeating began to manifest physically, as I was now introduced to a sedentary lifestyle for the first time in my life.

The changes in climate had a huge impact on me, both physically and emotionally, and I felt lonely, displaced, and greatly misunderstood.

Everything that I had known to be true was not anymore.

Life had become unpredictable and filled with more sexual, physical, and emotional abuse than I had the skills to cope with. So, food continued to be my friend; it was the only thing consistently dependable in my life.

Later on, in grad school, I learned about my underdeveloped emotional parts through the Internal Family Systems therapy model (IFS). These parts showed up immaturely in many of my relationships, especially when it came to dealing with conflict.

During the process to become a marriage and family therapist, I learned about Contextual Family Therapy by theorist Ivan Boszormenyi-Nagy; a metaphor of family relationships based on economics. The premise of this theory is that we are all born with ledgers and balance sheets. It assumes that people keep track of the debts or wrongs that have been done to them, and if those are not reconciled or forgiven, the next generation is subconsciously made to pay that debt in order to balance the ledger.

Nagy believed that whatever we are given by our parents, whether negative or positive, we pass it on to our children in order to balance our ledger. The same applies to what was taken from you, both positive and negative. We, in turn, take that from our children; also to balance our ledger.

In the African diaspora, this is known as generational curses.

"I will never do that to my children!"

This is a familiar phrase that was played over and over in my head. I might have even mumbled it under my breath a few times. Consequently, I made some vows; promising myself to do something different in parenting my children.

So, when my husband and I were blessed to give birth to three amazing children, I purposed in my heart to break generational curses, cycles, and everything in between. What I did not realize is that in order to discontinue a behavior, one must first be aware of that behavior, and take purposeful actions to make sure it's not repeated. Nevertheless, as hard as I tried, I still ended up repeating those I was not conscious of.

Watching my first born child and the only daughter grow up, I recognized that she was being made to pay my debts; as she also struggled with weight issues. I wondered if, through my experiences and what I had modeled for her, this had caused her to create invisible loyalties and destructive entitlement, in an effort to gain my love and regard. After all, she had learned to be loyal to what I was loyal to, and most importantly, she was loyal to me. It is a real possibility that she subconsciously began using food as a result of this loyalty. Her eating habits could also have been developed from her grudges and resentments towards me, which evolves feelings of entitlement which are destructive.

I became overcome with despair when during her teen years, her doctor ordered her to have a sleep study done. The result was that she has sleep apnea. It was devastating for me to pass on my CPAP machine to my teen daughter, causing me to question, "How could I have allowed this to happen?" "How could I have done this to my child?"

I was too familiar with the struggles of being overweight; yet somehow, I had also taught her to eat her emotions. I had vowed that diabetes and high blood pressure would not be a part of my legacy. Still, with the habits that I taught my daughter, this inevitably seemed to be her trajectory.

I had to confront my fears; therefore, I found and joined a 12-Step program that addressed food addiction, which helped me to confront the wreckages of my past and learn how to have a healthy relationship with food. Part of my zeal for working this program so diligently was to show my daughter (and my other children), a different way of living.

I wanted to be a living example of the solution.

I wanted to pay off my own debts.

Years passed, and I continued to desire deeper connections with my children; especially my daughter. In preparation for a difficult and necessary conversation with my now-adult daughter about how my parenting has impacted her life, I sought counsel from people in my support group, as well as from my core group of female friends; all of whom are on their own unchaining journey.

On that afternoon, I called my daughter and obtained her permission to have this discussion. During the phone call, I found myself pacing throughout our small apartment. I started the conversation by asking her, "What do you wish you had known when you were thirteen years old?" There was a pause on the other end, and then she said, "I really don't know."

I encouraged her to think about it; sharing with her that I know I made some mistakes as a mother and would like to repair them.

She said, "Mom, you did okay."

I encouraged her to dig a little deeper. So, she picked up one of her many journals, and as fate would have it, this was her journal from when she was thirteen. After turning the pages for a moment, she began reading one entry. Her words were bitter, piercing, and filled with resentment and truth.

Pacing the floor, I listened quietly:

> "...They tell me to keep in my feelings and opinions. What they don't understand is that there is already so much that I have kept in. I was brought up to speak my mind and not hold much back and talk to whomever necessary and open up.
>
> It's not that easy. What to say... what not to say.
>
> Can I trust them or not? I was taught these things, but when it is turned around, there are consequences now. If I tell them this or that, what will they say? What would they think? Should I even think about telling them anything? Will I get into trouble just for asking? What if I don't ask, but do and act-then things change. Now I should've talked to them... They are hypocrites just like everyone else."

Her words felt like hot wax being poured all over my body. As a mental health therapist, I knew that I had to check in with myself to assess what was happening in my body; I was flooded with so many emotions.

My pacing took me to the kitchen, and I wanted to reach for a box of ice cream or a pound cake. I wanted to eat something! Anything! I felt my thirteen-year-old self, struggling to break free; wanting to remove me from this situation, to protect me, and to be defensive and scream, "But, you don't understand!"

She wanted to explain what had been going on in my life at that time. Yet, as I continued to listen to my daughter, I felt her sadness and mine all at the same time. My thoughts drifted back to that fateful summer afternoon when I stood by that wire-covered tank in the middle of my yard, contemplating whether or not to jump in. In hindsight, I wished things could have been different.

I wished I had known a few things. I wished I had known that my uniqueness, my round face, my big forehead, big eyes, skinny legs and dark skin, were a gift to this world. I wished I had known that I was not a mistake, even though my conception might have been an accident. I wished I had known what love really looked like and how to experience it in a healthy way. This could have made such a positive impact on my emotional wellbeing.

So what happened to these wishes? During supervision to become a licensed therapist, I learned about our unfulfilled desires and wishes. I learned that they, in fact, are not erased or thrown into a sea of forgetfulness. I further learned that they follow us through life. Therefore, my best explanation of my wishes is that they became a penumbra, a shadow that casts darkness on that part of my life. This dark shadow has followed me through the different phases of my life; becoming experiences that have been unintentionally transferred to my children.

While I listened, I was grateful that I had enough clinical experience to reassure my thirteen-year-old self that she was safe, and to let her know that my forty-nine-year-old person would be able to guide and protect us both through this process and experience.

I snapped back into the present as I heard my daughter say, "I guess I wish I had known that my feelings were valid, that it was okay to express them, and also how to express them."

There you have it.

She had taken this script from the pages of my life. Whether I wanted to call it a generational curse, invisible loyalty, or distractive entitlement, it was time to address this.

No longer would I allow this silence to affect my family.

The cycle must stop here.

With the deepest compassion that I could muster, I said to my daughter, "I am so, so sorry that you experienced these things as a result of my parenting. Will you forgive me? What can I do to amend my actions?"

I could not defend. I could not deflect. I could not explain. All that I felt was necessary for me to do was sitting with her truth; the reality of her experience as it related to my contribution to parenting her. I shared with my daughter that I taught her how to eat her feelings.

She said, "I don't think you did, Mom. You did not tell me to eat something when I felt emotional."

I responded, "I might not have said that to you, but I've certainly demonstrated that for you. I was your example."

My body felt like a ton of bricks had been lifted off of me. I had come face-to-face with my truth... *and her truth*. I felt like a limp noodle, and I wanted to rest; my desire to eat compulsively during this experience diminished.

Her response was profound. She said, "I don't know what you can do, Mom. Maybe, when I have my own child, we'll figure it out."

I assured my daughter that, yes, we will figure it out together, and whenever she wants to revisit this subject, whenever she wants to talk about it, I am available; promising her that I will walk with her as she parents her own children.

What I do know for certain, is that I will be present to pay my debt so that it will not be charged to yet another generation; not my legacy. My children will not have to settle that debt with their children by passing on unbalanced ledgers. If I learn how to get what I need, then I will stop taking from my children and subsequently, my children will know how to get their needs met and not take from their children.

I've discovered that although I had repeated some of the same things I said that I never would, I truly desired to have a closer and more intimate relationship with my children. Most importantly, I wanted to free them to be the best parents they could be for their children; without the burden of my unintentional lessons.

Now, as I navigated this understanding, there were ten Awareness Keys that guided me through the ambiguity, fear, pain, and uncertainty of unchaining my legacy.

Awareness #1:
Acknowledging that I have made mistakes as a parent

Sometimes, it is difficult to admit that I am a perfectionist, but it is my truth. I try very hard to "get it right." Admitting that I've made mistakes, huge mistakes, as a parent was an important part of this process. Looking from the outside in, it might appear that I have this model family.

My family was intact; with two professional working parents in the household, and well-groomed, well-mannered, high achieving children, who made parenting seem easy. We were faithful members of our church and served in our community; however, there were many challenges and unresolved struggles that we had to figure out how to traverse.

These challenges and triumphs were not visible to the outside world, yet are the cords that bind us together as a family.

Awareness #2:
Owning my stuff without deflecting or blaming

When my daughter read from her journal, I felt my thirteen-year-old self, wanting to break loose and scream, "You are not the only one." That was not the appropriate time or context.

It was important for me to own what I had done (or had not done). Regardless of what was happening, or had happened in my life, during this conversation, my single purpose was to be present with my daughter in her truth.

My sole responsibility was to hold that space for her, validate her experience, and affirm her in the best way possible.

Awareness #3:

Committing to the unchaining process; no matter how long it takes or how difficult it may be

Committing to unchaining my legacy was not an easy process. I found it to be emotionally exhausting, at best. It was important for me to remember why I was doing this. The bottom line for me was to free my children from paying my emotional debts, and to stop taking from them; in order to balance my emotional ledger.

Their having a clean slate would create the opportunity for my grandchildren to experience optimal emotional wellness.

I also had to learn that this is not a 'one and done' event; this is a process that takes time and emotional investment, and I am not in charge of dictating the timing. Give others space and time, and be available when the time is right.

Awareness #4:

Being okay with the fact that there might not be a resolution

I've realized that unchaining my legacy is a continual process. The more my children mature, they might have questions, and I have made myself available to continue to share in the process of repair and restoration. I am also fully aware that there might be instances where there will not be a resolution.

Awareness #5:

Understand that people will be ready in their own time

Asking my daughter for permission to have this conversation was an important part of the process. It would have been selfish of me to expect her to be ready to explore this part of her life with me, just because I was ready.

In fact, if she was not ready to explore these challenges, I could have done more harm to her and to our relationship.

It was necessary for me to respect her timing and her pace. It was equally important for me to stay the course and be willing to see it all the way through.

Awareness #6:

Sometimes the things that I am trying to avoid manifests in different ways if they are not addressed

This awareness was critical. My voice was silenced as a child in many ways. I vowed never to do the same things to my children. As it turned out, I did the exact things I vowed not to. The methods were different, but the results were the same.

I have learned along the way, that in order to change a behavior, it is necessary to replace it with a different, more positive behavior. So, no matter how hard I vowed not to make the same mistakes, without intentionally learning new skills, those same mistakes are inevitable.

Wishing is not enough.

There is an assumption in the Contextual Family Therapy Model that is called invisible loyalties. This concept explains how one can be loyal to an idea, or person, subconsciously, so that they manifest the same behaviors to reinforce that loyalty.

Subconsciously, I was loyal to my upbringing and to my food; and ended up passing on the consequences of those loyalties to my daughter.

Awareness #7:
There must be a process of unlearning

I have made decisions and choices in parenting based on the things that I have learned; consciously or unconsciously. Awareness is key. Once I became aware, it was necessary to unlearn those things that did not serve me well.

The process of unlearning is not easy. Some things are ingrained and have become a part of my belief system. My unlearning process included my accepting that these things have happened, or are happening.

Prayer was important; asking God for guidance, wisdom, and knowledge. I have also had to replace what I have unlearned with new skills, positive self-talk, and different action. This has helped me to create new beliefs and behaviors.

Awareness #8:

Hearing the other person's truth from where I am now, but understanding it from where I was then

It was difficult listening to my daughter's experiences and truth. I was filled with guilt, shame, and remorse. I had to push through this in order to keep the process going.

I remember consulting with a friend who gave me this important piece of advice: She encouraged me to listen to my daughter's truth from where I was in life at that point, and exercise understanding from where I am now. I am not the person that I was at age thirty, or even at age forty-five. I have had new experiences, much personal and spiritual growth, and have also gained clinical knowledge along the way.

I empathize with my daughter's experiences, I also empathize with myself as a younger parent, and I empathize with my thirteen-year-old self. It might have been difficult for her to understand the choices that I made as a parent; however, I cannot defend those negative or unproductive choices.

I own them and seek to repair.

Awareness #9:

Forgiveness begins with me

There are so many things that I wish I had known when I was thirteen. If I had known these things, my life, and my children's lives, could have been different.

We may have had better emotional intelligence.

Nevertheless, I cannot change the past, but I can grow from it. In order for me to grow and have more meaningful connections in my relationships, forgiveness must be a part of the process, with forgiveness of self being first and foremost. This involves giving myself grace, which helps me to release perfectionism and the 'shoulda couldas.'

Then, forgiveness of those who I have learned from; realizing that for the most part, they did the best job they could, with the skills they had. They too have ledgers that they were attempting to balance.

Forgiveness opens the doors to so many healing possibilities. If I want to be forgiven, it is necessary that I extend forgiveness. In Contextual Family Therapy, this is known as exoneration. It is an important step in balancing my ledger.

This is still a work in progress for me.

Awareness #10:
Celebrate what I did well

This awareness key was difficult. When I am in the space of guilt, shame, and regret, it is hard to see the things that I have done well as a parent. Sometimes, it takes reaching out to people who have walked alongside me, for them to reflect with me some of the good I've done as a parent.

This reflection was also important for me and my daughter to do together. It was not an effort to minimize the mistakes that I have made; however, it was validation that I did do some things well. Yes, I lacked some critical skills, but I have also passed on some great ones. It is easy and almost automatic for us to be hard on ourselves, so celebrating me takes intentionality.

This process of unchaining my legacy has been about healing: spiritual, emotional, and physical. When we are burdened with guilt, shame, remorse, and UN-forgiveness, we create stressors in our lives that cause physical illnesses.

Some of these illnesses are anxiety, depression, overeating, or high blood pressure, to name a few. We use different substances in an attempt to fill the void that distant relationships have caused.

We are relational people. We were created for relationships.

Sometimes, the ambiguity of change can be scary and overwhelming. Unchaining my legacy has meant that I am creating a new normal for my family.

We are entering into uncharted territory.

Still, I welcome the challenge and the promise of increased emotional health throughout my family; both current and future.

"At some point in my life I decided, rightly or wrongly, that there are many situations in this life that I can't do much about - acts of terrorism, feelings of nationalistic prejudice, Cold War, etc. - so what I should do is concentrate on the situations that my energy can affect."

-Jim Henson; "Being Green," p159

Owning It

JANIKA N. JOYNER

"Tar baby." Black monkey." "Ugly."

Those were just some of the words I recall being called growing up. Words like that were not supposed to affect me. But they did. The phrase, *"Sticks and stones may break my bones, but words will never hurt me,"* simply was not true.

As a little girl, I was confused, because at home I was called "beautiful," "china doll," and "black beauty." Were my grandparents, aunts, uncles, and cousins lying to me?

I did not know what to believe.

In the back of my mind, I knew that I was something, but *what that something was*, I was unsure. When I looked around me, there were other dark-skinned kids; still, I was the darkest. I wanted to be lighter, I desired to be lighter, and I wished I was lighter. I began to view myself as *less than* or *deficient*. Something had to be wrong with me because my skin was so dark.

So, what did I do? I became the class clown, making people laugh, to hide the pain I felt by being called names and bullied... also, because I didn't want to bother my grandparents, who had taken on the responsibility of raising me.

Where was my mother? She was on drugs.

And, where was my father? He was in and out of prison.

I did not have my parents; an indicator that something was wrong with me. 'Proof' that there must be something wrong with me, right? I had to make up for how I truly felt and learned to "pretend" early on in life. Therefore, I pretended that the words and jokes didn't bother me, I pretended that I wasn't bothered when I found out my mother was on drugs, and I pretended that I was okay with my father being locked up.

You see, I was intelligent, and knew how to act.

And, that's what I did. I acted like I didn't care when I did; putting up a front and smiling when I was crying on the inside.

I was good at it too, or so I thought.

EARLY LIFE:

I was born November 21, 1984, in the Foundation Park area of Chesapeake, VA. Yep, during the infamous "crack epidemic." My mother was eighteen years old and a recent high school graduate. I was her first child, and according to her, she would "dress you up like a doll baby and change your clothes three times a day."

My mother did not use when she was pregnant with me; she said that she wanted to make sure I was healthy.

Thank you, Mom.

One of my earliest memories is sitting on the fence at the age of four or five with my mother teaching me how to snap my fingers. As far back as I can remember, my mother would pop "in and out" of my life. I knew she was my mother, but my grandparents raised me and my two brothers since she asked them to take custody of us.

When I was around five or six, I was introduced to my grandfather, James E. Savage, Jr. He would come to visit me monthly and take me to church, out to eat, and shopping. He told me I was special and treated me as such. I mean, he had my clothes made; treating me like a doll baby or a little princess. My grandfather was called "Doctor Savage" whenever we were out, and he always drove a Jaguar.

My siblings, and even some of my cousins said they wished he was their grandfather.

I knew I was blessed, because for a short while every month, I could forget that my mother was not around and that my father was in prison.

Fast forward to age eight... My mother would stay home for a few days, and then she would be gone for weeks at a time. We referred to these as her "missions." My brothers and I simply referred to her as "Dee Dee', calling our grandparents "Ma" and "Da" respectively. That is, until she put a sign up on the door demanding that we call her "Mom."

Maybe that was her way of saying she wanted us again.

I had friends who would speak about their mothers and their relationships with them: *"My mom and I were in the car and..."*

"My mom said this while we were in the hair salon together." My mom did not own a car, nor did she drive, but I still loved her.

She told me she used to go to school for nursing, but had dropped out right before she graduated because she was upset about something. I longed to live with my mother; wanting her to get her own apartment so that I could say "I live with my mom" and not my grandparents.

Do you know how much pressure is put on a little girl who has to answer why she is living with her grandparents and not her mother and father? I used to make up all sorts of excuses like, *she works too much*, and *she is sick*. I longed to experience living with my mom. What little girl doesn't want to have a relationship with her mother like the ones on TV?

I used to watch **The Cosby Show**, **Family Matters** and **The Fresh Prince of Bel-Air**. All of these families had both a mother and a father, and the daughters had good relationships with their mothers.

That's what I wanted.

Now don't get me wrong. My grandmother was a great mother, but she was not *my* mother. I felt like I was supposed to make her proud by getting good grades and not being a problem. Still, I longed to live with my mother; praying that she would get herself together so that she could come get us to come live with her.

Some nights, I would cry for her, but I kept my tears to myself and made sure I was quiet. I would cry for my father whenever I heard Whitney Houston's song, *"All the man that I need."*

This would go on until I was around nine or ten years old.

As a student, I would excel; ensuring that I made good grades. I wanted to make others proud of me because I felt the need to overcompensate for my feelings of inferiority, due to my life not being "perfect." How could I share that my mother was "in the streets?"

My grandparents did a really good job of raising the three of us. I have so many fond memories growing up. Good birthdays, Thanksgivings and Christmas. My childhood was filled with love, and I did not know I was "poor" until I got to college.

In middle school, I was inducted into the Gifted and Talented Education (GATE) program. I was able to go to a high school because I was smart and got called "teacher's pet" because I was smart and did not misbehave. Later, I was inducted into the National Honor Society. I did not think my mother would show up, but she did… drunk and wearing a suit with sheer pants.

Yes, sheer pants. The boys got an eyeful that night.

By the age of fifteen, I had a job, a car, and was living life. My mother would come around during breaks in her use.

We could always recognize when she was not sober, it was like she was a different person. Mean, cold, impatient, and hostile. She would give my grandmother money to hold for her at 5pm, promising that she was not going to come back for it; however, by 9pm she was back demanding that she be given her money.

This went on for a long time. And from that moment on, I had my mind made up that I was not going to depend on anybody or allow them to feel like I owed them. My dark skin and features had begun to garner attention from the opposite sex, and not those my age either.

I went from tar baby to "cute to be dark skinned." Now I was being desired by others *because* of my looks. They thought I was pretty, although I still didn't feel like I was.

Boy insecurity is something else!

LATE TEENS:

Around the age of sixteen, I stopped going to church and began to date "bad boys"; the drug dealers.

Not knowing *why* at the time, what I now understand as a Therapist, is that subconsciously I wanted to hurt those who had hurt my mother (of course, I knew that they did not sell her the drugs) and that was my way of getting revenge for her. I soon became pregnant and decided to keep my baby.

Boy, this devastated my grandparents.

However, I didn't make it to six weeks before I would have a miscarriage. Now that I look back on it, I feel as if that was a blessing in disguise. God knew I was not ready to be a mother; I was just a child myself.

The next year, I graduated high school and enrolled at Old Dominion University. My goal was to major in Criminal Justice and become a corporate lawyer.

That idea totally changed with just one Women's Studies course. I quickly realized that I could not live a lie; helping huge corporations make money, and potentially hurt hundreds, or even thousands, of innocent people. Therefore, I changed my major from Criminal Justice to Women's Studies. I became absorbed in learning about women in history and the oppression

and discrimination that women face, not only here in the United States, but also globally.

I wanted to help others, not knowing that I first needed to help myself. But until then, I decided that I was going to become a juvenile probation officer for girls; trying an internship at a Federal Probation Office.

That didn't turn out well, so I wanted to do something else; just *what,* I was not sure.

EARLY TWENTIES:

This was the era of being young, wild and free.

I was carefree... I had no kids, and I had my own vehicle, so I could go and come as I pleased. As a college student, I decided to leave home and stay in the apartments on campus; now able to experience what it was like to pay bills and be an adult.

And, as an adult, I legally gained entrance into the nightclubs. This little black girl now had curves, and my looks allowed me to skip the line and enter.

I became addicted. My confidence temporarily increased each time I was admired, complimented, and desired.

Still, I longed for something: to be complete and feel whole. I was searching for unconditional love.

My prayers were answered when I found out that I was going to be a mother. *Yes, me.*

Boy, was I in shock.

My doctor told me that I was due to deliver on my graduation date from Old Dominion University. The guy that I was dating at the time was just as happy as I was. When I told my grandparents, they told us that we had to "make it right."

So what did we do? We got married.

I had a shotgun wedding. We went to the courthouse with my great-grandfather as our witness. A couple of months later, he was locked up, and I was left seven months pregnant; raising my step-daughter alone and preparing to become a mother myself.

It was time to do what I did best... pretend.

This was not how I had dreamed and planned my life; a newlywed, yet a single parent. I felt ashamed, embarrassed, and guilty because somehow this was all my fault.

Then I got angry. Why didn't my mother teach me about this? She didn't know herself. Here I was, with no guidance and no real support because I had put up a wall, not letting anyone in aside from my immediate family and a couple of friends. I was so stressed that I delivered my son four weeks early; only six pushes and he was out.

No epidural.

I felt strong, but I was in shock. He was so little, so precious and so perfect. And, even though he was born early, he was healthy and did not have any medical issues.

Here I was a new mother, wife and lost. How would I keep my apartment and pay my bills? Graduate? Be a good mother?

My help came from the person I least expected.

My mother.

She moved in with me. It was a win-win situation. I finally got to live with my mother, and life would be great. Or, so I thought. My mother was still using, and she brought her boyfriend to live with us too. He helped out with the bills and worked. They used to argue a lot, but I ignored it because I had a live-in nanny; which would allow me to go and come as I please again.

Sitting at home, I felt lost, alone, angry and depressed. I needed revenge. And I would get it too. I was upset at my husband at the time for "leaving" me, so I was not faithful to him. I ran the streets even harder. Clubbing, acting like I was not married.

Yeah, that's how I got down.

I was not myself. I would work ten, sometimes up to sixteen hours a day, and then club all night. I was never home; either I was working or at the club or hanging out. I did what I knew how to do best. Pretend. In the club I was free, I had no worries, I didn't have to face the truth. But those lights would always come on, and then reality hit.

I had to go home.

You see depression is not just extreme sadness. For me, it was aggression. I was verbally aggressive and did not care about others or myself. I did not care what I said or did.

And, that win-win with my mother living with me didn't last long either. My mother started leaving and going on her "missions." She would leave on a Friday and not come back when it was time for me to go to work. I would have to call out because she was "missing in action."

I would allow her to come back, but only because I needed her to babysit so that I could go to work and to the club.

Soon, consequences would show me 'who's the boss.'

It was time for me to get ready for my husband's release, and I pretended that I had been a "good girl" who had been patiently waiting for him. He knew I wasn't, but went along with it anyway. After a while, I came out and told him (after being caught) that his son could possibly not be his son. And guess what? He wasn't.

That was a very difficult time for me. Talk about shame, guilt, and embarrassment. This man that I married believed that my child was his first-born son.

I had messed up... big time.

I even tried to run and hide; yet, I couldn't avoid the inevitable, and we were divorced.

This pattern of me being afraid of failure and disappointment was starting to get old. Attempts to live the "perfect" life were failing, and I will tell you why. I kept ignoring this voice telling me *Janika, I love you unconditionally. Flaws and all.*

I ignored that voice and put on my pretend face again.

I became the "great pretender" and started working longer hours and multiple jobs to keep myself busy. The busier I got, the lower that little voice would get. I was always on the go and traveling out of state: Charlotte, Atlanta, New York, etc. I was "single and ready to mingle" all the while bottling up all of my emotions. I was living the life once again... about to graduate with my Masters this time.

Although I felt horrible as a person, awful for confusing my son, and a failure because I had ruined my marriage, I continued to stay busy; it kept me from having to face the truth. Something had to change. I could feel it. I just didn't know what. I completed my first-year internship in a substance abuse program, and when I finished, I told my mother, "You need to go there."

We sat on my grandmother's porch after one of her "missions," and she told me she was tired. Guess what? She decided to go.

Not only did she keep her word, but she also went to therapy and started going to NA groups. She attended groups every day. My mother stayed clean for 30 days, 60 days, 90 days, 6 months, 1 year, 2 years, 3 years, and now... 6 years.

Her getting clean set me free.

No more shame, no more guilt.

I finally got my mother back!

PRESENT DAY:

One day, I finally listened to that voice, broke down in the mirror and said, "Janika I forgive you."

I think I cried for about two hours that day.

When I was done, I was an ugly mess. But, I felt good. I felt free. I felt like a different person.

The second thing I did that day was to ask God to forgive me. I prayed and asked for strength and courage to face my fears and walk in my purpose; knowing that I was no longer the same insecure and lost person. I was okay with myself and wanted more.

I deserved more.

After all, they say, *"You do better when you know better."*

Following graduation, I worked at a cemetery for about six months, and then I became a therapist. I found something that I was good at that allowed me to feel good about myself. I began dating again too.

Nothing serious though. I wasn't looking for love; I was working on Janika.

I also started going to church more.

That felt good.

After some time, I became serious with a guy and decided I was ready for a steady boyfriend. Life was not perfect in this relationship because I still allowed some of my "old ways" to creep back up whenever I became uncomfortable. Nonetheless, he saw something in me that I did not see in myself.

He knew my past... I mean all of it. And, I knew his.

We accepted each other, flaws and all. Then, I became pregnant, and we split up.

Lord, I don't know what I was doing wrong. How could I have another failed relationship while expecting another child?

This time, however, instead of doing what I was used to, I began to pray. I asked God to lead me, I practiced forgiveness, and we were able to work it out and remarry; vowing to stick together through the good and bad times, and agreeing to not keep secrets.

I realized that I had struggled with allowing him to "be a man" as I was "Miss Independent"; putting on my cape and acting as if I had it all together. I also recognized that I emotionally kept my husband at arm's length out of fear.

Thankfully, he was patient with me. Patient as I figured out how to love myself and accept that I could not change the past. He wasn't going to give up on me, just as my mother hadn't given up on her sobriety.

For once, I began to feel complete.

Each time I had attempted to find love in "all the wrong" places, God showed me that his love for me would surpass anything that man could give me, that he loved me unconditionally, and that he could make me whole; even in my perceived brokenness.

My life is still not "perfect" as no one's life is. However, my struggles and past experiences have shaped me into the woman that I am destined to become, and I am okay with that. Life has obstacles, and there will be times of disappointment, but they do not define me.

When I said 'yes' to God and began to show up for Janika, my life changed. The following list helped shape my next steps, which ultimately led me to open up and want to share my story:

- Stop comparing yourself to others.
- Your past does not have to dictate your future. You are the author of your story.
- We ALL make mistakes. But, when we do, we must
  1. Learn and
  2. Grow from them
- Be patient with yourself and others. Change does not happen overnight.
- Forgive yourself first; then seek the forgiveness of others.
- Take care of yourself: you can't pour from an empty cup.
- If your decisions are not safe and healthy (for your mind, body, and spirit) don't do it.
- Your story is your story, so why would you allow someone else to tell it? In order to heal, we must be real.

- Don't be afraid to ask for help. No one can do everything alone.
- When all else fails, Pray!

Let this chapter serve as my first endeavor to practice what I preach. I am *"Owning It,"* and hopefully you will have the courage to own whatever your "it" is as well.

This process in itself has been liberating.

You see, my legacy is not fully unchained. The links are just beginning to separate.

Stay tuned...

Feelin' Some Type of Way

ILLIONA ILLY OKEREKE

"There is a reason the windshield is bigger than the rearview mirror. Your future matters more than your past."
~ Max Lucado

I remember that day vividly. My dad was sitting at the top of the staircase, looking down at me. The hallway was dark, with just a little street light peering in, so I could see his face; as he told me not to tell the cops what happened. I was scared out of my mind, but I think part of me was just tired of it all.

Years before this moment, some of my earliest childhood memories included seeing Marie being dragged on the floor by her baby's father, Peterson. She was completely disheveled, crying, and yelling. They rented a room from my parents, but I guess Peterson felt like, "Hey, they're just the landlords," so it didn't stop him from physically abusing her.

My mother probably was scared herself, but I couldn't tell. My father attempted to intervene, and sometimes he was successful, but other times Peterson saw him coming from a mile away and waved him off. I don't remember if Peterson lived there or not, but it's almost like the only time I remember him being in our home was when I heard the sounds of Marie crying in agony.

Some years later, my parents purchased another two-family house in East Orange, New Jersey. This time, we lived upstairs, and there was domestic violence on the floor beneath us.

An African American couple, parents of two young boys, always seemed to be yelling and fighting. Of course, we never saw much of what happened from upstairs, but the next day or so I would see Tanya's black eyes, welts, or bruises. She always walked out of the house like nothing had happened the day before. If my father came knocking on the door, Tanya would defend Quincy and say she did not need help. The beatings got so bad that even neighbors came over to try to help.

One day, someone ended up calling the police, and Quincy was taken away in handcuffs. They moved out of the first-floor apartment shortly after he was released.

Until my pre-teen years, my childhood was plagued with domestic violence. Marie and Tanya weren't the only women I saw go through this. As a young child, I witnessed my mother being physically abused at the hands of my father.

It's been approximately 20 years since the night when my dad looked down at me in the hallway, asking me to keep his secret, and at least one of the scars from that day still remain on my mother's body. So, I didn't have it in me to lie to the police officers. Matter of fact, I think I sang like a canary.

I don't know what happened between the night he was arrested, and the day he was released, but I didn't get into trouble with my father for reporting him. From that day forth, he never hit my mom again, but no one sat me down to talk to me about my thoughts and feelings.

Was I confused? Frightened? Angry? Was my little brain able to appropriately process and cope with what I was experiencing?

Life just happened, and we kept moving on; feelin' some type of way, but not talking or doing anything about it.

My parents bought this new house around the time my father had just gotten saved. This was a big transition for all of us.

My mother, younger brother, and I left our old church and started attending my dad's new church. He was at home more often than he had been before this change in his life. Therefore, his presence created tension in the home that was not previously there.

The physical abuse stopped, but the emotional abuse didn't.

We became better acquainted with his quick temper and the frustrations he primarily took out on my mother, and on me, secondarily. He intentionally made remarks to hurt my mother's feelings; criticizing everything she did. He called her names from stupid to inappropriate words not worth repeating.

Though his new-found faith convicted him of continuing to physically harm her, those convictions did not extend to his mental and emotional abuse towards us.

My mother was highly anxious about trying anything new and often doubted her capabilities. She stayed in this abusive marriage with my father because she did not believe she had a choice. As a Haitian immigrant navigating the American life with two children and possessing limited English, as well as a limited ability to write or read in any language, she believed she had to endure to survive. She is one of the toughest women I know.

Aside from my father's hands, it is remarkable that I only remember seeing my mother cry two other times. In the mid-90s, my parents flew to Haiti for my grandfather's funeral. As I watched the VHS tape of the funeral, my mother was stoic the entire service and even during the walk to the burial site. When the burial ceremony ended, my mother lost it. She wailed out the loudest, inconsolable cry I have never seen her display since.

The second time she cried was at my grandmother's funeral last year; over twenty years after her father's death. My mother endured her hardships through prayer, attending church services, and just keeping busy.

My mother had dropped out of school at a young age when my grandmother got ill so that she could take care of her younger siblings. She compensated for her lack of education through memorization and the use of context clues. Her ability to manage money well was a great benefit to her family in keeping up with their immediate needs.

Without much of her mother's assistance, she learned much of her life skills on her own, and she did what she knew well.

On top of acclimating to a new country and culture, my father's criticism disrupted her worldview and shattered her self-esteem. Learning new things, no matter how vital was anxiously provoking because she did not have faith in herself. She continued to do what she knew best which was to stay busy and take care of others. She was feelin' some type of way, but she never really talked about what or how she felt.

Unfortunately, I learned to cope with life in similar ways.

My father, on the other hand, was an unruly child. He took on his father's temperament; often described as a 'hot head.' Though he was very charismatic and humorous, his anger was just as infectious. For most of his childhood, he traveled between his mother and father's house until he became too much for either of them to handle. He was sent to live with his uncle, but ran away because my father thought he was too strict.

Though my father rarely hit me, I sometimes wish I had those wounds instead of the emotional ones. I remember his silent treatments. There were a few days when I asked my father, *"Can you take me to church? There is a youth service happening."* I don't know why I even bothered. I already knew what his response was going to be.

Our new church had stricter rules than my parents had and I tried to follow them... for the most part. I wasn't going off to a club, trying to wear big hoops earrings, or rebelling against any random items on the "don't" list. I was really going to church, yet he would just sit there... in silence.

It was obvious that he heard me, but he would not respond. I was fearful that he would yell at me or beat me, so I had to find my own way to church, and anywhere else I wanted to go.

I often functioned in a parental role, instead of living out my childhood. It was my responsibility to make sense of everything that came my way and my parent's way. When bills came in the mail, I read them and interpreted them for my parents. I wrote out the check and mailed it out on their behalf. I talked to bill collectors and translated at important meetings or appointments. These were my responsibilities on top of my household chores.

As for academics, I had to figure out homework on my own. There was no older sibling to help me out except my godbrother for a short period of time. If it was wrong, I didn't tell anyone because they couldn't help me anyway. I just learned from my mistake and tried harder the next time.

I was also in after-school care, but I didn't feel they were helpful since I thought I already knew what they were trying to teach me. My mother then placed me with a babysitter who saw how reliable and helpful I was, so she often had me take care of the other children. I told my mom she was wasting her money, and if I can take care of the children there, then surely I could take care of me and my brother at home alone.

I was encouraged and rewarded for being self-sufficient at a very young age; indirectly taught that it was okay because it made my parents proud at how much I was able to accomplish on my own.

I understood my parents' financial situation to a degree, so no one had to work hard to buy me things I needed for school or keep me up to date with the latest fashion trends. I saved and earned my own money so that I could buy what I wanted or needed for myself.

That is how I coped... when I was feelin' some type of way.

There was a time in my life that I was at church six or seven days per week. Once, while the leader of the dance ministry, I held a rehearsal that took place during a blizzard. I went to pick up one of the dance members, and while following my father's instruction to drive slowly and carefully in the snow, we headed to the church. Halfway there, the wheel spun out of control, and my car landed horizontally in the middle of the street.

It felt as if my heart fell out of my body, yet I kept driving to the church anyway. I look back at that now and think, *I don't know what any of us were thinking. I would never let my child do that.* I had just gotten my license and even adults were not driving around in that amount of snow.

I am not sure if there was an important event coming up, but in my mind, it must have been urgent. The truth is, it does not matter what event was coming up. I needed to be at church. It was my safe place. It was my escape. It was one of the places I felt not just accomplished, but also appreciated. Like my mom, I could be "busy" being a caregiver. It did not matter if I was on the pulpit or behind the scenes. Being involved and engaged in the community in some way was its own reward.

The church was a consistent place of re-parenting for me. The youth and youth leaders helped me to really connect with God and even to make education a priority. While I did not have much support or encouragement from my parents about college, I received it through talking and watching the people in my church at the time. They inspired me and are the reason I took the college process so seriously.

During my sophomore year in college, my family moved to Florida. They always asked me when I would move down with them, but my new school and church was my safe place. With a four-year scholarship, I could not leave to attend a new college and rack up extra school loans.

They did not understand how college, scholarships, and transfers worked, so as I had always done, I had to figure out things on my own. I had to stay focused, so I did not even have the time to grieve the loss of my family moving miles away. I was feelin' some type of way, but I didn't really talk about it.

Every once in a while, I visited my family in Florida, but there was one time in particular that my father hit me with the silent treatment. I was so undone. What had I done wrong? What had I said to get in trouble? What could it possibly have been? I could not understand. Then, it dawned on me; my flight was the next day. My father felt some type of way. He was upset that I was leaving and he did not have the emotional vocabulary to say, "Nana," as he affectionately called me, "I will miss you."

Instead, he relied on his natural bend, which was to distance himself. And, to his surprise, I responded to his cold shoulder with a warm kiss on his cheek.

He melted like butter.

I know it was not my responsibility to teach my parents how to properly emote. In fact, it was their job to teach me. Still, I wish I had known earlier what I found out in the moment I kissed my dad. My father loved me. He just didn't know how to show it. He had not been raised that way, and his brain was not wired that way. However, I have peace with my understanding of his dysfunctional language of love. I just want to cultivate a healthy legacy of love with the next generation to come.

Though I gained a better understanding of my dad, I did not have any level of understanding of men in my teenage and young adult years. My parents did not allow me to have male friends growing up, so I did not really know how to be (just) friends with a guy and therefore I dated a few guys who mistreated me. Sometimes I did not grasp the gravity of a situation until much later because my self-esteem and self-worth were pretty low.

I thought Kordell was going to be the love of my life. We had a lot of the same interests, but it was our mutual love for music that bonded us together. We were inseparable, enjoying each other's company and did almost everything together.

Despite the fact that I was rough around the edges and communicated abrasively, he still stuck around. I can imagine that while some people may have thought we were the cutest couple, they couldn't imagine how a guy that was so calm and kind-hearted would date a young woman like me.

Some people even hinted that if they heard we had a disagreement, it was always *my* fault, and *I* was the one with the problem. Kordell would chime in with the unsolicited opinions of others and play the role of victim. It was a toxic relationship that recreated similar dynamics of my relationship with my father. He took out his frustrations on me and had me wondering what I did wrong? How did I mess up this time? The anxiety was overwhelming.

I felt some type of way.

It took me years to recover from the relationship.

In one of my graduate courses, we were required to go through counseling for a minimal time period and document our experience. It was the best thing I had done in my life. In the first two sessions, my life forever changed. We explored some of my childhood, but most of all how it was immediately impacting the way I dealt with life. This was when I was instructed to use a feelings chart to help me identify and express my emotions.

This exercise was extremely difficult for me because I didn't usually talk about my feelings. I usually just let life happen.

In that time, I often heard my peers say, "I'm feelin' some type of way." This was the phrase we used to indicate that we're aware (and we want you to be aware) that something is going on emotionally, but we rarely sat with the feeling nor took the time to really describe it.

That certainly was not what my therapist was looking for. She wanted to know the exact type of way I was feeling.

Scared? Anxious? Lonely? Shame?

Through our time together, I began to learn how to help others enter my world of emotions and to become acquainted with it myself.

I was not on the journey alone though. During my graduate school years, I was living with one of my pastors, Lily, who was like a second mom to me. She, along with friends, and other spiritual leaders was instrumental in re-parenting me. They helped to bridge some of the cultural and intergenerational gaps I had with my parents by initiating important conversations and asking questions that challenged my worldview. They recreated a family dynamic that provoked me to communicate, fight, and love better – even with my own family.

A few years after my family moved to Florida, my father was in and out of the hospital. Though he knew how detrimental his actions were, he continued to eat irresponsibly and had not taken good care of his health for years. He had several strokes, was on dialysis, and in addition to battling diabetes for the last decade, he was diagnosed with coronary heart disease and glaucoma.

During one of my visits to Florida, I noticed that one of my father's pupils seemed a little glassy and didn't move. I asked my father about it, and he indifferently told me that he was blind in that eye. My father's health had been getting worse, and no one was communicating with me about it. I was feelin' some type of way, but this time I was going to say something about it.

After encouragement from Lily, I told my mother to let me know if/when she believes that my father's hospitalization becomes serious. In Creole, she said, "I'll let you know, but every time he goes to the hospital, and I think he's not going to make it, he always comes back."

I had no idea.

A few months later, in April, she called to let me know that my dad was pretty bad and that I should come see him. I went down for a week, and he was asleep every day except the day before I was about to return to New Jersey. He was shocked that I was there. His speech was limited, but I was able to talk to him for a few short minutes. Approximately three days later, my mother called to tell me that my father was gone and the life support was the one breathing for him. She requested that they remove the respirator the next day.

My father died on April 21, 2011. Of course, I was feelin' some type of way, but life kept moving. I had to fly back home to take my finals. I also had to do something about how I was feeling though, so I went away to the beach.

Prior to my father's passing, he had made amends with my mom. He repented of his treatment of her throughout the years. He confirmed some things she had already known, and he shared some things she did not know. She said she forgave him wholeheartedly and had no angst towards him.

That warmed my heart.

I went to counseling the following year, but three years after losing my father, I found myself in my office crying and hyperventilating. I was burdened with grief and sadness. My support system helped me get through that day; however, I realized that despite my best efforts, I struggled to sleep through the night, my hair was thinning out every year around the anniversary of my father's death, and I got diagnosed with several food allergies and digestive issues. My body literally grieves my father's loss and damages from my childhood upbringing. I have hope though. Significant changes continue to take place in my healing journey.

I am so appreciative of my husband, Emmanuel, who has played an instrumental part in my healing. My mother-in-love raised him well. Emmanuel is not just my husband, but my friend... my best friend. I feel safe being vulnerable with him in every way. Spending quality time with one another and having our weekly 'date nights' help us not only maintain intimacy, but provides us both with the mental breaks we need in life. He sends me gentle reminders that I am human and that it is okay to "be" and to "feel."

So, it's not okay to just feel some type of way, but it's important to express what and how I feel in our safe space.

We did not always have the best models of healthy marriages growing up, but we are committed to having a lifelong, healthy, and happy marriage. Therefore, we surround ourselves with healthy individuals and married couples who possess similar values. We observe, listen, ask questions, and have serious discussions because we want to a build a solid foundation for the next generation. We want to unchain a legacy that fosters mentally, emotionally, and spiritually healthy children.

What I have learned from my own childhood experiences and working with children and adolescents is the importance of the following:

1. **Self-Awareness.** Be aware of, in tune with, and consciously make efforts to maintain your mental, emotional, spiritual, and physical health. This includes being aware of who and what triggers you and setting the appropriate boundaries.

2. **Self-Care.** While children are a significant priority, parents/caregivers cannot fully and adequately take care of their children if they don't take care of themselves as well. Taking time out for yourself is not a selfish act. It is maintenance so that you can optimize your ability to

serve as a caregiver. Meditation, exercise, massages, and therapy are among various self-care tools that can be utilized.

3. **Reach out and Receive.** There are a lot of us, strong women out there, but none of us need to be strong *all the time.* By reaching out for help, it takes the pressure off to be superwoman and reminds us that we are human.

4. **Support System.** Be around people that bring out the best in you and challenge you to be the best you, but who can also handle you at your worst. Surround yourself with people that are committed to growing with you and helping you whether you know you need it or not.

5. **Safe Space.** In addition to having your own safe space, be the safe space children have to emote and express their feelings.

6. **Model.** Modeling healthy behaviors, even when recovering from your own mistakes or hardships, are integral in teaching children how to cope with life. They are already watching what you do so be mindful to practice what you preach.

7. **Balance.** Teach children life skills, age appropriately, yet allow them to experience being a child. We live in a microwave generation, but a child's brain is not built to

develop at that same rate. It is important for parents/ caregivers to set the pace needed for children to grow, learn, and live in the moment.

8. **Be Fully Present.** At the end of the day, kids don't need perfect parents; they need present parents. Not just physically present, but actively involved in making their best efforts possible. Talk to them. What are they thinking? How are they feeling?

Though I wish my parents were able to teach me how to properly cope with life as a child, I truly believe they both did the best they could with what they knew. While I did not learn these important lessons in the past, I am learning them now and will be able to teach them for the sake of my own life and legacy. As in Philippians 3:13, my focus is no longer on my past, but rather I look toward the future.

> *"But one thing I do: Forgetting what is behind*
> *and straining toward what is ahead."*
> ~ Philippians 3:13b

Their Forever Mom

SABRA STARNES

*"She realized her desire for belonging
was her soul asking her to love herself."*
~Jaiya John

Every year infants, children, and older teens have parents who relinquish the right to be their legal parent, and this leaves the child parentless, and it is then that a family that is either blood related, or non-blood related, is found.

There are about 1.5 million adopted children in the United States; which is 2% of the population, with 140,000 children adopted each year in the United States.

I chose to be a mother through the adoption of my two sons. Why? Because I am also an adoptee; having experienced both the pain *and joy* of adoption.

My story is about being able to give a foundation of trust, vulnerability, and security for my sons and my 10-month-old granddaughter. As their mother, my greatest hope and wish is for them to have true happiness with themselves and with others.

There are many misunderstandings, misconceptions, and myths about adoption that can be overwhelming for an adoptee; which can lead to depression, distrust of others, loneliness, and living a life of unhappiness.

Before I decided to adopt, I worked on these to be prepared to be the mother my sons deserved and needed after their mothers relinquished their maternal rights.

Several months ago, I decided that it was time to share my adoption story, and I am glad that I did. It has been a journey of intersection, acceptance, and a better understanding of how my adoption journey has impacted my life and given a greater awareness that I am changing the narrative of my story for my sons. For reference, when I say my sons, they are my adoptive sons; on the surface, I think of them as my sons, not my adoptive sons, and to the world, I often keep that private. Not as secret, but private, because it is their decision to tell it, not mine.

I made a promise to them that I would let them tell their own story when they were ready. However, in writing my story of motherhood, I include how I became their mother. And, with their permission, I am sharing a bittersweet story of destiny and fate of how my own family was created and how I then created my own family. In giving my sons *me*, I made a lifetime commitment to both of them that I would celebrate our union and honor their birth family, even if much was unknown, but that I would be there when they were ready to search on their own for their birth family and any information.

I want to start with what being adopted means first.

Adoptees can experience relinquishment at birth or the involuntary removal from their birth mother due to neglect and abuse. This disruption is emotionally and physically traumatic for the child, and does not go away once the child is placed in a permanent home; the adoptive family. It has been well researched and well-studied, that the first three years of life are critical for the infant to have a safe and secure attachment with their mother. And when the child has experienced a safe and comfortable bond, the infant learns that they are safe and secure with their caretakers. This is where we all learn, "I can get what I want. I'm safe, I'm provided for; I'm important".

When the mother abandons their child emotionally and physically, this is when the infant or child no longer feels nurtured and a part of a family. The messages the child then begins to receive is "I'm not safe; I'm not important; I don't matter."

Both of my sons were removed from their birth mothers (they are not birth brothers) due to neglect and abuse at the age of three years old. There were many attempts and hopes for their birth mothers over the next three years to get their sons back.

But, it never happened.

They remained in the foster care system; made to wait and wonder if anyone was going to come and adopt them. The wait for the child can be short, or it can be years. For many years, children languish in the foster care system, because they were in limbo, they didn't have their parental rights terminated, in hopes the parent would do what was required to get their child back.

And then, there is the fact there are not enough people who wanted to adopt. This left children to have to grow up not knowing if they were ever going to have a permanent home.

Adoption is still very misunderstood by people because no one has asked an adoptee about being adopted. Many people think of "Little Orphan Annie" being adopted by a rich man and all her worries of being adopted where gone.

Yet, that is not that case for the millions of adoptees who deal with the pain of feeling unwanted, unloved and thrown away. When you are adopted, it doesn't erase that you had a birth family. The loss of knowing where and who you came from affects your self-identity and sense of self-worth. I would have preferred to not have been adopted, but to have been with my birth family.

Each adoptee deals with their adoption issues in different ways. The issue of abandonment by the birth mother leaves an ongoing fear of abandonment for the adoptee. In my experience, if the past abandonment issues are not healed and released, it can cause ongoing pain for the adoptee throughout their life.

Understanding how adoption negatively affects adoptees has been a personal and professional quest for me as an adult.

What I have learned through experience and working as an adoption therapist for the past 20 years is that adoptees deal with issues of trauma, self-identify, loss of power that can lead to low self-esteem, loss, and grief, attachment and relationship issues due to not being able to trust others.

My life work as an adoption therapist has been both challenging and rewarding in helping adoptees and adoptive families to develop secure, healthy and loving relationships.

What makes a mother, anyway?

A mother, according to the venerable Oxford English dictionary, is a woman who has given birth to a child; a woman who exercises control like that of a mother, or who is looked up to as a mother. Motherhood is the condition or fact of being a mother; the spirit of a mother; the feeling or love of a mother.

When I was 30 years old, I was ready to be a mom, before I was ready to be married or have a career of my dreams. Yet, I wanted to be the best mom... no, the perfect Mom. I often felt very alone and worried that raising two boys would be too difficult for me to handle, and it was hard to accept that I would make mistakes, not always get it right, or not always say the right things as their Mom.

I love my adoptive family, but I don't love that I was adopted. I love being an adoptive mom, but I don't love that my sons were in the child welfare care system. In sharing my legacy about adoption, I want to share what I have never shared with my two sons because like me, they had been abandoned by their birth family. In adopting my sons, I have never erased their life before me, pretending that they were better off with me than with their birth mothers.

When I adopted my first son as a single woman who had just turned 30 years old, I was often told how lucky they were to have me adopting them. That was the worst thing to say to me. It was not luck that brought my sons into care due to abuse and neglect.

I will never forgive their mothers for how they treated my sons. I have never wanted them to think or believe that they were not loveable, so I gave them all I had and more to make sure they knew that they had not been thrown away and abandoned.

My adoptive parents had done the same, in all the ways they knew how, for myself.

Nevertheless, like most adoptees, being adopted can leave you feeling incomplete as a person; as if something is missing.

As an adoptee, I often have felt stuck; stuck between wanting the birth family I didn't know and adoptive family I had. My relationship with my adoptive mom growing up was strained. I desperately wanted to see her in me, but that never happened. I was often mad at her and felt she loved my sisters and not me.

As an adult and more importantly as a mom, I get it.

In my case, growing up in a transracial adoption, having white parents and a white sister, it was obvious that I was not my parent's natural child. Still, they did a great job of never making me feel like I didn't belong or was not their real child.

And, I now know that my belief that my adoptive mom loved my sisters more than me was coming from my fears of abandonment; often causing me to feel unlovable and detached from my adoptive mom.

On the other hand, I would make them feel that they were not my real parents; especially my mom. I remember saying, "you're not my real mom" to hurt her feelings when I was upset or sad.

As I grew up, my family would always share that as a family we would do the search and reunion of my birth family together. I fantasized about my adoptive parents, older adoptive sister, and twin sister walking the world together until we found them. I wish I could say that is how it happened, but it didn't. I also wish I could say that it will be easy for my sons to find their birth family, who live in the same area that we live in, but it won't be.

Even in the age of technology, social media, and Google, people can still hide and not be found

I always believed that if I could find my birth mom, it would be the closure that I needed to truly know who I was; and it would also be what I desperately needed to heal from the pain of being abandoned at birth.

As a young adult, I began going to therapy to work on finding out who "Sabra" truly was. I struggled with accepting myself for how I looked on the outside and how incomplete I felt on the inside. At this time in my life, I still didn't know why my birth mother had relinquished her rights to be my mom at birth; and the pain of having to assimilate into a white family, and a white community, left me feeling confused and alone.

Much of the pain of being adopted is losing a part of oneself at birth in the separation from the birth mother and never feeling whole. Much of the healing is to attempt to feel whole again by discovering one's true self.

This can be a harder and longer developmental process than for the non-adoptee. By releasing the pain of adoption, we have found our authentic selves - that adoption is a part of who are - but we are *more than* our adoption story.

Then, when I was 21 years old, we found my birth mother, and she wanted the reunion with me and my twin sister; giving me an opportunity to be in a relationship with her for the next eight years. Our relationship ended as it had started... with her abandoning me as her daughter. This time, it was because she wanted me to forget my adoptive family and be thankful for all she had done for me. After she told me this, I was furious and reminded her that it was my adoptive parents who raised and loved me, not her.

I had made myself a promise that I was committed to keeping, that I would never let her leave me again.

So, this time, I walked out of her life. I never thought I would have had the strength to do this. The mother that I looked just like and acted just like, I was leaving her.

I lived much of my young adulthood angry and acted out because I didn't have the words for the pain I was feeling. I often felt like I lost my true self, and a lot of times I felt like I was living a facade. I struggled with the joy of loving my family and the pain of being abandoned. When I had finally found my birthmother, it helped me to feel for the first time truly whole and complete; an African American woman whose parents were white.

Although my search and reunion did not end the way I had imagined, I now live with the realization that she only wanted to be found by me, so that she could live out her façade that she had never given me up at birth.

After the difficult closure with my birth mother, I began to think about becoming an adoptive mom. I knew that I was ready to be a mom, so I took the classes and became a licensed foster and adoptive parent. I received mixed support on my decision; losing a few friends. And, my parents were concerned that I was too young to adopt children.

However, I followed my heart and knew that God would bring me to my sons... and my sons to me.

In looking back over the sixteen years as their mother, we have come a long way as a family. We have been through a lot, but I never gave up on them.

The first time my oldest son called me mom was at church. We had gone up to the pew for prayer, and I was asking for strength and guidance in raising him because I felt so alone and unsure of what I was doing. I had little support, or everyone told me, "You're doing great," but what I needed was help as a new mom. However, since he was 6 ½ years old and not a baby, no one came running to pick him up and hold him when he cried and screamed, and wanted the foster family he had been attached to for the three years before he came to be with me.

I remember kneeling at the pew as I prayed and prayed, and cried hard and painful tears; my son looking at me like I had lost it. The pastor came over and prayed with and for us, asking my son, *"Who is this next to you?"* He said, *"My mom."*

It felt amazing.

My youngest son was in the same foster home for three years until he came to stay with me. I knew I wanted to adopt again after adopting my first son, yet I waited two years before going through the adoption process a second time. The local child welfare agency called me and asked if I would meet a little boy, but I said *no* because I thought I wanted a girl.

God always knows what is truly in our heart.

I felt a strong tug at my heart to call them back and say *yes*. I met my youngest son for our first visit on a Monday, and he was with me on a Friday! When I met him, I was just as scared and nervous as when I first met my oldest son. My youngest son quickly attached to me; calling me mom the moment after he met me. Each child will attach differently, and just as I had done with my oldest son, I provided security and permanency from the very beginning.

His foster dad was a seasoned foster and adoptive parent, but he was no longer able to care for my son because of his age, and his home had become an unlicensed foster home.

Adoption will always be a bittersweet way of becoming a family; for the child, the birth parent and the adoptive parent. And there will be children who like me, were given up as an infant, or like my sons who languished in the foster care system until an adoptive family was found.

Both of my sons have shared that I have saved them from a life that would not be as it is now; not perfect, not with their original family, but it is secure and constant. I want to be their steady always, as they have gone from young boys to teenagers, and now young men. I want them to know that they're not alone or unloved. Nor, do I want them to think that because they were adopted that their story is that and no more.

I have given them a life of love, security, and trust in allowing them the power to choose me as their mom. Everything I have done since I have had them both has been for them to be able to know they had me. I don't want them to ever forget their birth mothers; they gave them life and loved them.

My sons are stronger and emotionally healthier young men because of my determination and commitment as their mother. And, I am the woman I am today, because of my sons. I am truly blessed to be their mom; and to my sons, they are my true purpose in life. I can't imagine not having them in my life.

Monster in their Eyes

MICHELE MIKKI JONES

"You never believed me."
"I don't hate you; I just don't understand you."
"He was a monster, but you were a bigger monster."

I'd be telling you a lie if I said that each statement doesn't hurt. They all do! Each one bears its own kind of gut-wrenching, heart-breaking pain that is truly undeniable. But, denial is exactly what I once lived in. Oh, now you see me all back straight, head high, voice strong and confident; not taking shit from no one, and giving tea for the fever; even if you don't like it.

Yet, can you take this journey back with me from a time when my back was laid flat from the abuse I suffered as a child? To a time when my head hung so low that suicide seemed my only option? To a time when my voice was silenced by the pain that I had endured? To a time when ugly was the only thing I saw when I looked at me?

"You defeated your purpose."

No harsher words have ever been spoken to me by my mother. In that one terrifying moment of her drunken truth, at age 24, I finally realized why she had always hated me so. The look of disgust in her eyes at the very sight of me helped me to come to grips with the pain of the beatings she inflicted at two in the morning. Those words "you defeated your purpose," released me from the embarrassment I felt at seeing her drunken naked body as I guided her home from the middle of the street.

Hearing her say those words "you defeated your purpose," freed me from the mental anguish of knowing that "I love you" would never come from her lips to my ears.

And, the distorted acceptance of her willful blindness to the pedophilic deeds committed against me by her boyfriend - that she never believed - I knew there would be no absolution. Right now, in this instance, in her drunken clarity, I now understand why I've lived the last two decades of my life in a living hell.

Now, here I stand, tears streaming down my face as she speaks to me; having rescued her more times than I can remember, having put her to bed more times than I care to count, having endured her abuse on more occasions than I care to share, and all she can say is that I've defeated my purpose. Well now, because I am not one to languish in pity or be defeated by opinion, I took that moment to dry my tears and use it to motivate my every move that followed. I was determined to prove to her, and all who would listen, hear, and see, that I do have purpose... and that I will not be defeated.

Ha, who the hell am I fooling? I was so fucking miserable that it wasn't funny. The only thing is, I didn't know it. And, for the next eight years, those four words "you defeated your purpose" ruled my life.

The promiscuity that followed was unbelievable. I found myself walking around with an STD questionnaire, and if you answered my questions, then you had a 10 out of 10 chance of taking me home with you. At the time, I seemed to have a stomach of steel, and a constitution of stability, because alcohol was my best damn friend. I was a hundred and five pounds and could drink a two-hundred-pound football player under the table; having him crying for his mama.

By this time, I had four babies, two miscarriages, and three abortions. I didn't need a soul in my life but me, myself, and I... and my children. I was quick to tell you that "promises are lies made to be broken. So, don't make me any promises, and I won't tell you no lies."

I partied in every state surrounding New Jersey and then some. It would be nothing for me to call my Grandmother and ask her to pick up my children for me, or to leave them with my god-sister for days on end. It wasn't until one night, sitting at the bar with the same drink in front of me for at least two hours, feeling the weight of depression and tiredness, when an old friend came in, sat down beside me, and made me smile.

Funny how I recall the beginning of that night now, because this same man that made me smile, tore the rest of my broken soul to shreds when he raped me.

That terror, the tears, that fear that I felt at the age of ten was back again at the age of thirty-two. I had no one to turn to, no one to talk to, and no one to help me through. I didn't trust any female to understand. I didn't want to feel any comfort from anyone; woman or man. Stay the fuck out of my life. Leave me alone.

Give me my kids and my job, and get the hell away. Don't knock on my door, don't ring my phone.

Bitches be GONE!

Yup! This is where my MONSTER began! I had these misconceived notions about how to avoid pain, and I had all of my best-laid plans mapped out, only to find that, up until this very moment, they had been laid all wrong. So, at thirty-three, I switched gears, and I got married.

HAHAHA – what a freaking joke that was! As I look back in hindsight, there were these subtle hints that something might not be quite right with his playful attention. I deluded myself into thinking that it was just my overprotective imagination because there was no way that I was going to let my daughters go through what I went through; to be like my mother, and not see it.

I know what the abuse looks like.

OOOHH the lies we tell ourselves. It is impossible for you to "know" what sexual abuse looks like!

Why not?

Because no two offenders look or act the same.

As an abused child, I had developed this tunnel vision view of - if he does this, he says this, he acts like this, and it only happens when this - Straight bull shit. I was a child then and had no idea of how ANY of THIS was supposed to occur. What ten-year-old do you know that understands mom's boyfriend is NOT supposed to take you out of one bed, put you in another bed, and lie down behind you; getting your pajamas all wet? What twelve-year-old knows that your cousin is NOT supposed to touch you like that, and then tell you *"SHH, don't tell nobody."*

Surely, not anyone that I know.

But, what made matters worse, was that I had run away only to get caught in the same situation all over again; in a place where I was supposed to feel safe. If I had to give an accurate count of the different males that had abused me from the ages of eight to thirteen, it would be six. And that doesn't include the rape when I was an adult.

So, when your thirteen-year-old daughter stands toe-to-toe with you, in the midst of an argument about why the heck she is doing everything that you are telling her not to do and yells at you, *"That's why your husband is touching me,"* OH HELL to the NAH! My defenses immediately kicked in, and instead of going for him – I go for her! I damn near jumped across the banister to strangle the crap out of her. How dare you bring to light the fact that I didn't protect you! How dare you stand in my face and say to me the very thing I wish I had the courage to say to my own mother! How dare you have to endure the same pain as me, and to have me not know how to help you!

It was not until I went to therapy that I had to accept that this was the exact moment I had become the *Monster in Her Eyes!*

The venom in those eyes; I sometimes still see it to this day. Not as intense, but evident just the same.

This can't be happening! Are you kidding me? How the fuck did I miss this? IMPOSSIBLE! I did not just repeat the very thing that I despise my own mother for! Did I just hear her correctly?

And, because I didn't want to hear, refused to hear, and wouldn't hear, I responded in an inappropriate manner, and things just got worse. Because I never went for his throat, I had inadvertently given him full range and free access to mess with my daughters; fucking us all up for life. It was a total nightmare living in that place, in that space, for the next four years.

My eyes were so blinded by guilt and pain that I missed shit that was obvious to a blind man.

The coping mechanism I used was church. I became so immersed in the church that I again neglected to protect my children. Never doubt the viciousness of people for the sake of religion; they can be extremely cruel and unkind. My hope was that God would somehow cleanse his soul and make it all go away... wash it with the Blood and cover us with grace and mercy.

The lies we tell ourselves when we have no valid excuse for STUPID. However, it seemed like the more I prayed, the more he preyed. Another mechanism was work. I worked two to three jobs, just to avoid the fact that I didn't live up to the expectations of motherhood, and had ultimately failed at being a parent.

I set up rules and gave curfews, while my girls laughed at me; behind my back *and* in my face. They had people around them whispering in their ears "your mom is evil," "your mom doesn't care about you," "you don't have to listen to her"; and they believed it.

As much as I wanted to say SHUT THE FUCK UP! to every one of them, to some degree, what they were saying was true. If I had known how to care enough, the marriage would have ended that night on the stairs. If I had known how not to be cold-hearted, evil would have never found its way in, and I sure as hell would not have thought that staying was the best thing to do.

If I had known how to listen, I would have heard my own voice first. And, while I am now in a place where I OWN MY OWN SHIT, POOH to my sisters and brothers that stood by and said NOT A DAMN THING!

Fuck you and the high horse you rode in on.

Because of your jealousy towards me, your vision was just as clouded; causing you to be part of the problem and not the solution.

But I digress. Because even knowing what I knew about my eldest child, exactly when I became a Monster in my middle daughter's eyes — I don't know! I will not say that she came out unscathed, because she has her triggers that remind her of her experience. I do know that her rebellion was the worst, which only added more fuel to my guilt and shame.

I didn't know what to say to rein her back in, so I just shut her out. I couldn't help her or her sisters, because I had yet to help myself. I didn't know what to do or say, because the only guide I had, was no guide at all. Therefore, I dealt with the rebellion of my daughters, as if that night on the stairs had never happened.

Again, my denial was real and my marriage still intact.

The impact of all the pain that I had allowed to fester in us became clearly evident to me when the DYFS (Division of Youth

Family Services) Worker showed up with the police at my front door, to investigate allegations involving my youngest daughter.

At first, I was thrown off, because the worker was someone I knew, and clearly, they had the wrong address. But, when the police officer asked for the ex by name – OH SHIT!

Here we go again. For years after the incidences, we – as a family unit of me and the girls – had not discussed the abuse, nor addressed the emotion that went with it.

Still, the girls had been talking about it with everyone except me… and now the police were knocking at my door. And, here's the kicker, my daughters were more upset that whoever had told, had betrayed them just as much as I did, and they literally wanted to cuss everybody out.

There were so many telephones calls, and so much name calling, that you would have thought the scene in front of my house was from a longshoreman movie. My daughter was cussing like a sailor and couldn't be stopped. The quiet came when they too recognized who the DYFS worker was.

Because the DFYS worker couldn't involve herself in the investigation since she knew us on a personal level, she immediately called her supervisor to recuse herself, and the next day a different worker came out to interview my youngest daughter. It was during this interview that I realized that I had also become a *Monster in Her Eyes.*

She had to relive that whole experience in the presence of strangers, and once again, I was not there to protect her. I was not allowed in the room to be part of the discussion because they needed full disclosure, and I was an externally negative influence.

WOW! The gravity of that statement still stuns my soul to this very day. Suffice it to say, that this is the catalyst that put him out of the house.

This would also be a good place to tell you that my choices just kept getting worse. My delusions of normal were so *abnormal* that I had fooled myself into believing that now that the testimonies were recorded, the investigation was concluded, and the documents were sealed; that all was right with the world again... that time heals all wounds.

Such sacrilegious bullshit!

Nothing in the world was right, and just because the investigation was closed, it didn't mean that the incrimination was over. We still had to contend with "the family secret." But, at least he was gone, and the house had calmed down. That was until I bought the house we called 'The Wood' and let him move back in.

Long gone was the shame related to the physical aspects of the abuse. Now, its all-encompassing evil had been eclipsed with feelings of resentment, guilt, and pain. My daughters hated him, yet they hated me more. I hated him and was hoping that he hated himself.

To this day, I don't think he ever has.

What I do know is that 'The Wood' is where I finally got knocked over the head with the voices of my children.

It took two more years in a marriage that was nine years and 364 days too long; nevertheless, I finally unclogged my ears and listened to what was being said. 'The Wood' is where my double ones (my granddaughters) were born, and I'll be damned if I was going to give him full range again; to spend another major part of my life turning a blind eye.

NOPE! Not even gonna give you that chance.

I had to finally let it all go.

The marriage was over, and I had to understand that in order for me and my daughters to heal, I had to acknowledge that HE DID IT, but I needed to OWN my part in IT!

- Own the fact that I had never admitted and accepted that I was sexually abused as a child
- Own the fact that, as a mother, I did fail to protect my daughters
- Own the fact that I (we) needed professional help
- Own the fact that the bad choices that I made as the adult adversely affected those around me
- Own the fact that I had disrespected and ignored the feelings of my children and transversely chose a demon over them
- Own the fact that if I wanted to rid our family of the monster, I needed to rid our family of the old me

Consequently, the divorce came, but my foundation with my children had been destroyed. Rebuilding it has taken time; forcing difficult conversations to be had. I had to sit back, shut my mouth, and eat every word that my daughters spit at me.

Not because I didn't have a defense, because I did. But, because they needed to say it, and I needed to listen.

I had already begun the process of forgiving myself, but that didn't mean they were ready to forgive me. See, that's the intricate thing about forgiveness; while it may be for you, it still has to be given. I first learned this lesson in rape counseling, and I ignored it. It came up again in divorce counseling.

This time I paid attention.

2009 was a learning curve for me. It was when I really understood what it meant to accept responsibility. It was when I looked in the mirror, disappointed at the person staring back at me, understanding the monster I had become, and getting help to deal with it, instead of running from it.

Therapy helped.

I went to therapy to forgive those who had abused me when I was younger, and the mother who refused to believe me. I went to therapy to come to terms with the impact of the rape. I went to therapy to formulate a plan to finally be there for my daughters; whenever they decided to begin the process of forgiving.

I now know that to them, at times, it still feels as if I am being distant when in actuality I am making strides and putting forth the effort to get closer. To them, it sounds as if my tone is condescending when in actuality I am still learning compassion.

Before I owned my own part and started destroying the monster I had become, I was broken and hurt, tied down with guilt and shame, and standing on a weakened foundation; the proverbial house of cards.

One strong breath, one sleight of hand, and everything about me would have fallen to pieces.

In fact, on several occasions, it did.

My first suicide attempt was at 24, my next was at 32, and my final was at 39. My daughters don't even know about them. However, through the healing and forgiving process, I had to learn that failure is the flip side of success, and in order to succeed, I needed to fail.

Now, the catch is that I get to choose what I fail at. I didn't know that then, but I understand it now. I cannot go back and re-see all the warning signs that I missed. I can't go back and be a better parent. I can't go back and take the hurt away. I can't go back and fix my mistakes. And, I can't go back and tell all the "bystanders" that "my daughter is telling the truth!

STOP CALLING HER A LIAR! She is NOT EVIL!

The monstrous choice all those years ago was not that I married a man who had depraved, unnatural, thoughts and actions. It wasn't that I ignored all of the warning signs (although it didn't help), but it was that I stayed. Even after hearing what was said, and seeing how it had affected my family, I did nothing. I buried my head in the sand; refusing to see life for what it was. I forgot to put on my big girl panties on that fateful day, standing in the hallway at the bottom of the stairs, seeing the pain in my daughter's eyes, and wishing it away like I had done my own.

In that one pivotal moment, with that one hesitation, and with that one instance of reflection, I was the *Monster in Their Eyes*.

Hindsight is 20/20, and my vision back then was seriously fucked up. I have come to see all of my missteps, apologized for those that I knew about, and repented for those offenses that I had no idea I had committed.

Which is why, when my daughter called to tell me about something that had happened to my granddaughter, and when my response was not something she wanted to hear, *least of all from me*, I knew exactly what she meant when she said, "I don't even know why I called and told you." Guess what my love – don't lie to yourself like that. You know exactly why you called me. You called and told me because you wanted to hurt me. You called and told me because you wanted me to see what a "real" mother's response should have been. You called to tell me because you wanted me to know that you were a better woman than I was.

And, my response to her call was to apologize for my initial reaction, and tell her to *"listen to your daughter."*

Thank you for taking this journey with me. The person I was then is so not the person I am today. I have witnessed my own evolution, and am proof that people change – and for the better. I will no longer stand idly by; saying and doing nothing.

Not for mine. Not for anyone else's.

This is why I know that in order for me to break the cycle of generational sexual abuse, and to build a legacy that my daughters and granddaughters can be proud of, I accept full blame for my part in the past; vowing to use it as a foundation for the future.

And, here's why:

- I am human
- I am not perfect, nor is perfection my goal
- I am fallible, and I make mistakes
- I am learning compassion
- I have a voice that needs to be heard

- I have a story that I need not be ashamed of
- I cannot be held accountable for the actions of others
- I will be held accountable for my actions (or inaction)
- I have a responsibility to myself and others
- I will not remain a victim, even though I have been victimized

I know that I am not alone in this. I know that this didn't just happen to us. I know that you can't just make this shit up!

More importantly, I know that it is hard to reconcile the pain, the regret, the anguish, and the guilt. And, because I know this, I also know that rebuilding is possible; as long as it is done on a healing foundation.

The past cannot be erased, and as much as we would like to forget, that is not always a possibility. The one thing that is probable, is the growth that occurs from the past will leave one with the strength, the courage, the fortitude, and the voice... to rebuild all that pain has destroyed.

Own your truth, and never let your truth keep you bound.

Rewriting My Life Story... From Rags to Riches

TEARANIE WILSON-PARKER

"The opposite of a profound truth
may well be another profound truth."
~Neils Bohr

If my life was made into a movie being played out on the big screen, in viewing my early years, one would realistically determine that the legacy I would leave to my children and all those I may influence would be one of poverty, abandonment, abuse, and shattered dreams.

The profound truth is that my life began in chaos. I was born to a young mother who had dropped out of her second year in college because she got pregnant by a gifted and talented artist who was heavily addicted to drugs. I remember the story my mother would often recall of how she had to flee from the only home she knew, to give birth to me because her mother refused to have anything to do with her; that is, until I was born.

Also, I would hear about how she was shunned and disgraced; and hence my entrance into this world was not surrounded by love and joy, but tears and pain. In fact, my name... "Tear-anie" pronounced exactly like the word 'Tyranny', was chosen because my mother shed so many *tears* when she was pregnant with me.

Therefore, it would be reasonable to say, that due to my chaotic beginning, I was destined to live a life of limitations, brokenness, and despair.

For some reading this chapter, your life began in disorder as well, and therefore, the legacy passed down to you should also be clouded with turmoil.

Or, should it?

If you asked one million people what 'Legacy' means to them, you would hear similar and diverse answers. While some would say that legacy *embodies monetary wealth and valuable possessions*, others may say legacy *constitutes values, traditions, character traits, or meaningful life lessons that were received from parents, grandparents, or other ancestors.*

But, what does legacy mean to you? Is your meaning similar or something entirely different? In contemplating the word 'legacy' as it relates to my life, my thoughts are flooded with the heritage that was handed down to me and my siblings.

The good, the bad, and the ugly.

The profound truth is that the legacy we inherited does not fit the mainstream definition of wealth and valuable possessions, nor was it one of family traditions or life lessons. Our legacy was gift wrapped in chains. However, amazingly, my mother did instill in us the importance of obtaining a good education and the power of prayer.

Yet, is that a legacy? If poverty, abandonment, abuse, and shattered dreams can transcend multiple generations, then the opposite of that profound truth may well be another profound truth... that both good and debilitating things can pass from generation to generation, but any debilitating part of that legacy can also be altered.

When I realized this truth, something remarkable happened; it was as if a light bulb went off in my head. An 'AHA' moment! And then, another revelation came that was just as riveting. The only thing standing in the way of a more desirable legacy materializing into existence was *me!* Not my past, not my unfortunate circumstances, not other people. Therefore, the ONLY thing that may possibly be standing in your way is... YOU.

Let's take a trip back in time. It's the late 1970's to early 1980's and my siblings, and I are living with my mother; a single parent of four children.

Our father has been in and out of our lives for years. He was a talented artist who could draw just about anything, and one of my fondest memories of him was watching him paint beautiful pictures with all of his paints and brushes situated around him. Unfortunately, I also remember the drugs and his strong addiction to them; a vice he could not shake, which caused him to miss great opportunities; both personally and professionally.

My father did not have a college education, but he had been in the military for a short period of time. Remarkably, I don't think I have ever known him to have a steady income. Feeding his drug habit was his full-time job. So, it was not uncommon for him to disappear for a few years and then suddenly re-appear into our lives. I remember my father telling me years later, how he had hitchhiked to California, from Florida and back.

Not once, but several times.

After ten years of marriage, my mother finally divorced him. Although he did not provide a steady income for our family when he was married to my mother, it is no surprise that she still did not receive any income after they divorced. Eventually, his addiction led him to be diagnosed with AIDs and dying in his mid-50s.

To sum it all up, no child support for four children, with nothing but a high school diploma, and living in public housing where drugs and crime were woven into the fabric of the community. Living in this type of environment, we were destined to become a negative statistic.

On welfare, baby mama drama, constant lack, fragmented souls from abuse, brokenness from abandonment, and addiction to drugs was the legacy that should have materialized in the earth realm regarding us.

The one thing that BLOCKED this legacy from taking root was the power of prayer. The profound truth is that prayer will unchain the legacy that was purposely designed by God for you and your family to walk in. Prayer will pull truth from the spirit realm so that it can be birthed and 'appear' into the earth realm.

Prayer will allow you to 'see' yourself as you really are... royalty, the head and not the tail, above and not beneath, one with authority to expand territory and transfer ownership of that which God has destined for you; even if the circumstances around you are the complete opposite!

Therefore, the truth is that any destructive part of a legacy can be 'unchained' due to the power of prayer.

Now, let's fast forward to today. My two sisters, brother, and I are now adults with our own families. We have been through a lot as children; however, like some of you who are reading this chapter, we do not look like what we've been through. In fact, even some relatives in our family are dumbfounded and can't believe how well our lives have turned out. It just doesn't seem possible, that children, who were raised in such a traumatic environment of poverty, sexual abuse, and abandonment, now wear love, forgiveness, hope, and faith as armor.

However, the life that we now live has not been handed to us without a fight. We have had good and troubled times. But, now we have children and nephews (no nieces as of yet), and the legacy that will be handed down to them, and those we influence, must be vastly different from the one that tried to chain us.

Clearly understanding what needs to be 'unchained' for the next generation is a must.

In going back to the meaning of legacy, I stated earlier that some would say legacy embodies monetary wealth and valuable possessions, others may say legacy constitutes values, traditions, character traits, or meaningful life lessons. Regarding the legacy that has now materialized in our lives and will transcend generations, is one of faith, hope, character, tradition, fulfilled dreams, and the power of prayer. However, when it came to my life, there was still one area that was much harder to overcome, and that was *poverty*.

Merriam-Webster defines poverty as:

"The state of one who lacks a usual or socially acceptable amount of money or material possessions."

Poverty not only may entail a lack of financial resources, but also an impoverished mentality. Although I have exceeded the financial means of my parents, I always had this feeling that I should be experiencing more. I was able to 'see' and 'believe' for greater abundance, though it had not yet materialized in my life; yet, I strongly believed it had to be more than merely having *just enough*. However, I had a serious problem, a poverty mentality.

I was equipped with financial knowledge, but my impoverished mentality encased invisible barriers around me and obstructed opportunities for financial increase. Having *'just enough'* and living paycheck to paycheck is still a form of poverty. Unless we realize this, we will not change unhealthy financial behaviors and walk in complete abundance, fruitfulness, and multiplication.

Since a damaging part of my legacy was poverty, it was destined to be my portion and could have possibly been passed down from generation to generation. Nevertheless, there are scriptures that I often quote and meditate on:

"But remember the Lord your God, for it is He who gives you the ability to produce wealth, and so confirms His covenant, which He swore to your ancestors, as it is today."
~ Deuteronomy 8:18 NIV

*Those who work their land will have abundant
food, but those who chase fantasies
will have their fill of poverty.*
~ Proverbs 28:19 NIV

Well, I was working my land, but I was also the borrower, who was a servant to the lender (Proverbs 22:7). My poverty mentality had opened the door for repeatedly getting in and out of debt, spending money I did not have on materialistic things, and living beyond my means. The root of this was insecurity, which stemmed from childhood issues.

I would remember the times I went without when I was a child, and that would trigger the need to overcompensate for my children, because I didn't want them to feel the way I had.

For instance, at the beginning of every school year, I had to make sure they had new clothes and several pairs of shoes; all name brand items, because I remembered being teased for not wearing popular branded clothes or shoes.

Let's not even discuss Christmas and birthdays; I would get into so much debt making sure my children had a lot of gifts. The amount of money I would spend for that one day a year, every year, took me years to pay off.

Where I grew up in public housing, my children lived in a four-bedroom home in a middle-class neighborhood. I didn't have much as far as clothing and shoes, but my children had more than enough. My mother and father had only a high school diploma; yet, I have a master's degree. My mother had one car, where I have several cars. I was raised in a single parent home, but my children were raised in a two-parent home; not experiencing abuse, abandonment, or rejection.

So, from the outside looking in, it does not appear as if poverty would be their portion. Still, if I don't teach them about making prudent financial decisions, nor tell them about the financial mistakes I made so that they don't repeat them, then granting the legacy they inherit will be different from mine, there's no guarantee that they will not squander their inheritance and continue in the same cycle.

Therefore, as I look back, I realize that buying my children these things was not just for them, but it was for me as well, because I didn't understand that emotional childhood trauma can affect you financially, years later, if it is not dealt with.

However, I 'see' so much greater for not just myself, but my children, and all those I am called to influence. Just having enough will not cut it and although my children's life is better than what I experienced, it's still not what God has destined for them. The profound truth is that God wants us to not only be good stewards of what He has given us, but He also wants us to multiply it as well from generation to generation.

Ensuring that my children had more than I had was not an unreasonable desire. However, unchaining my legacy should consist of more than just leaving monetary wealth. It is also about teaching my children and others how to steward well and multiply their money. How can I afford to leave an inheritance of life insurance, investments, and savings, if I am giving all my money to creditors?

Thus, breaking the poverty mentality had to begin with me, and I was fortunate to marry a man who did not have the same hang-ups with money, which helped a lot.

Nevertheless, even though I was being healed of the emotional trauma from my childhood, I soon learned that my soul was fragmented, and I not only needed inner healing, but also to become whole; mind, body, soul, and spirit.

I didn't know it at the time, but overcoming poverty was something I was indeed destined to do, because eventually I became a financial advisor and started my own movement called **Funding an Empire**; proving that your greatest challenge can be turned into your greatest victory, if you 'see' through the eyes of faith, instead of being influenced by your five senses. What you 'see' in the natural can change, but it's entirely up to you.

What is even more amazing, is not only did my money habits change, but so did the money habits of my mother. My mother had been a young mother, whose life had not gone the way she dreamed. She was always living in survival mode, and she did not express the desire to build and leave a monetary inheritance to her children. It was not until recently when she began to 'see' the importance of leaving an inheritance to her children's children that it became her goal.

I can remember a time when she didn't want to talk about life insurance because her mindset was, "we were trying to get rich off her death."

Now for some, this may sound a little off, but for others, this is something you also have heard.

Thankfully, the truth is that the destructive part of a legacy can change... her mindset has changed as well; which has occurred through receiving financial knowledge, and hearing others talk about the need to leave an inheritance to heirs.

My mother now lives in a home she purchased, she has eliminated almost all of her debt, and she is good with saving money. Even though my siblings and I are all adults, she is still teaching us that financial mistakes can be corrected and that your past does not determine your future.

What about you? Do you or did you battle with a poverty mentality? Was this or will this be a part of your legacy?

A poverty mentality does not have to be generational; the choice is yours to unchain. Even if you obtain a lot of financial knowledge, if your mentality does not change and you continue down the path of making financial decisions that keep you in poverty, or for some, staying at the same limiting financial level as your parents, then the next generation may repeat the cycle. So, how do we unchain a legacy of poverty (of just having enough)?

To answer this, I have outlined some helpful information to support you in unchaining your legacy... and that of generations to come.

1. You have an empire! Since the opposite of a profound truth may well be another profound truth, clearly understand that this is another profound truth. Your empire could be a business, a professional career, a military career, a ministry, and even a family. A family?

Yes, because you need a steady stream of income to achieve short and long-term family financial goals.

Funding your empire can consist of having a financial plan, savings, investing, saving an adequate amount for retirement, business profits, rental properties, having multiple streams of income, health insurance, long-term care, and a suitable amount according to your goals of life and disability insurance. To continuously and efficiently Fund Your Empire, there are KEY components you can't leave out; it's like baking a cake... you can't only have flour.

Therefore, in funding your empire, you also need to consistently manage your money properly. Poor money management will literally cripple your empire. It doesn't mean you will not make financial mistakes, but it does mean that you don't have to continue making the same financial mistakes over and over again.

2. Identify and address any childhood issues that may be hindering your ability to take advantage of financial opportunities. Are you fully aware of the obstacles that may be hindering you in achieving greater levels of financial success? Is it procrastination, a lack of financial knowledge, or fear? What negative thought patterns do you need to change? What are the psychological triggers that cause you to make poor financial decisions?

Don't let the little girl or boy inside of you control how you spend your money. Some of us are living at or above our means and therefore, limiting our financial potential. Eliminating or limiting debt is a great start. There are so many debt reduction/elimination plans available, choose one, and stick to it. It's just that simple. There is no magic pill or magic solution; you must be determined not to be a slave to the lender.

If you leave your children your home, and it has liens against it due to debt you have incurred and not paid off, then the amount of money they could inherit will not only be eaten away by taxes (we can't always avoid that) but also by creditors (we can avoid that). Remember having the right mindset changes results.

3. You must have a CLEAR picture of where you are financially, and what financial strategies are needed to get you where you need and want to be 5, 10, 15, or 20 years from now so that what you have built will be a great part of your legacy. Time is the one thing you can't get back. Therefore, what can you do today, that will allow you to literally step into the future, and alter the financial destiny of your children/grandchildren?

Think about that for a second, and then I want you to remember the legacy that was handed down to you. Is it something you are proud of and desire to leave to your children/grandchildren, or should you begin, or continue, to change any part that is undesirable?

4. Entrepreneurship must be incorporated. As a child, I often heard this phrase... *get a good education and then a good job.* However, I believe that we should leave a legacy of entrepreneurship, as well. Some of our children will not go to college and earn a four-year degree. Some may not have the mindset of working a 9-5 for some company. Some will have jobs, or some may go into the military, but their salaries may not bring in the income they need and desire; therefore, we need to expose them to more... owning their own business(s). I wish someone would have encouraged me when I was young to own my own business.

    Is owning a business for everyone? No, it is not. You must work hard, be consistent, and continuously develop industry knowledge and marketing skills. However, we still should expose our heirs and those that we influence to becoming business owners. We should also expose them to the concept of having multiple streams of income, as well as, encouraging them to become avid readers. There are so many great books on leadership, self-improvement, entrepreneurship, and finance. Wouldn't it be awesome if our children and grandchildren read books that will help them grow both spiritually, personally, professionally, and financially?

Here is another thought-provoking comment - Instead of dying without a Will, what if we leave a legacy of having a Will and/or Trust created, and having all family members present to go over what will be distributed to who, how the funeral and burial expenses will be paid, and what will be passed down to family members regarding family traditions, life lessons, and family values. Now, this may not stop family members from fighting over money, land, and possessions; but it can eliminate arguments between sisters that believe the furniture in their mom's house was really meant for one and not the other...all because their mother's true intentions were never clearly communicated.

The legacy that you inherited may or may not be one you want to be repeated throughout time. The question I want you to ask yourself is, *"what part of your legacy needs to be unchained?"*

Will financial knowledge, monetary wealth, and valuable possessions, along with life lessons, traditions, faith, and family recipes from your great-grandmother, continue to be passed down to the next generation? Have you, or are you, funding an empire, and do you want to ensure that your family understands what it took to make the money you worked so hard for and will leave to them?

> **"A good man leaves an inheritance**
> **to his children's children..."**
> ~ Proverbs 13:22a

Will your legacy emphasize that the current generation should teach the next generation how to continue traditions, life lessons, and various ways of generating wealth while creating new ones?

Bottom line, debilitating cycles do not have to be repeated, and you do not have to be defined by the situation you were born in. You can re-write your life's story; passing down wisdom in making financial decisions as well as the resources that can increase generational wealth.

From rags to riches.

Now that, my friend, is a legacy that is truly unchained!

I Swear I Heard God Laughing

TONYA RENADA MOORE

"Trust in the LORD with all your heart and lean not on your own understanding; In all your ways submit to him, and he will make your paths straight."
~ **Proverbs 3:5-6 (NIV)**

Woody Allen had a saying, "If you want to make God laugh, tell HIM about your plans." Making God laugh seems to be one of my greatest accomplishments. Even when I take painstaking steps to plan my future or events, careful to work out every minute detail, the one thing I almost never consider is:

What would God think or say about this?

The story I would like to share involves the relationship between me and my youngest child, Jasmine. However, before I go into the sometimes funny details, I'd first like to give you a brief history of me and my son's relationship. I always knew I wanted a son, and when I became pregnant, I claimed it. As luck would have it, that was God's plan too.

I shall call my baby boy, Jacoby.

At the time of Jacoby's birth, his dad and I had been dating for approximately five years. I was twenty-four years old when he was born, and his father and I never married.

From where I stand, Jacoby is the best part of his dad, and although his dad and I didn't raise him together, eventually, (and it took a long time) we became friends.

From the beginning, I believed it would be just the two of us forever. I wasn't delusional, however; I realized that one day he would grow up and become a man, eventually marry, and have a family of his own. At the same time, I never saw my own future or how it would look. I never imagined being married or having more children, but I did make one declaration... if I ever did have another child, I would be married first.

As a young adult, I never thought I would marry. Who would put up with my attitude? Well, here's where God starts to laugh. I met my husband, Carlos, when Jacoby was six years old. We were married a year later. In my opinion, my husband is a great dad to Jacoby, and I believe my son loves and respects him as a dad; although never forgetting his own dad.

When I was 32 years old, I gave birth to my second child, Jasmine. My husband and I agreed we wouldn't have any more children, as two was plenty. He said that after the minor complications I had during delivery, he didn't want me to go through anything like that again; however, secretly, I think he didn't want to share his love with any more children, and that somehow he would be "cheating" on Jasmine by dividing his time and attention with another. I believe in his heart that he felt Jasmine was the best thing that ever happened to him. I waited a few years just to be sure before we made the decision permanent.

Weeks after Jasmine was born, she began to come into her looks; she was the spitting image of her dad. Try as I might, I could not find any physical resemblance of me. Sometimes, I stared for hours, but there was not one thing I could find, to say I was a part of such a beautiful baby. If I hadn't given birth, I would swear I was not even in the room when she was born.

Recently, Jasmine and I were at a store getting her eyeglasses ordered. A woman working in the store said to me, "You two look just alike." I said, "Oh yeah? You're only saying that because you haven't seen her dad." She was sure I was wrong. "No, you two look so much alike, I could tell she's your daughter."

I said to her, "Okay. Well, we'll see."

My husband walked in, and the lady's mouth dropped open. She looked at them both and said, "I stand corrected, I have nothing else to say. Wow! I can't believe how much they look alike. It looks as if he spit her out." We all just got a big kick out of this, because we've heard that same statement a million times.

In my mind, my daughter was the prettiest baby born in the world in 1999, the five years preceding, and the five years following. Now, there might have been some cute babies born those years, but they didn't hold a candle to my Jasmine. She was a very smart, bright, and happy baby. She learned to walk at eight months, and her personality at that age was something I could not have imagined.

There was little doubt she loved her father with all her small might, and she loved her mommy the same. She didn't play "favorites"; sharing her love equally between the three of us... me, her dad, and her big brother.

Even as a toddler, she showed signs of being a unique individual, and was determined to be her own person. She was already a good person, always tried to do things to impress and please us. As she got older, she cared about people's feelings, and I never remember hearing her say one bad thing about anyone.

Fast forward to her teenage years, and God is laughing even harder. Jasmine had always excelled academically, enrolling in either the talented and gifted programs or honors classes, and receiving anything less than an "A" was unacceptable; it hurt her feelings. She also received the President's Award for Educational Excellence signed by our first African American President of the United States, Mr. Barack Obama.

What an honor! My baby girl had a brain!

Around age fourteen, I started noticing a change in her personality. My kids have never been in trouble outside our home. I'm not bragging, just stating facts. They are successful, and I have to think I played a small role in their success. I added some ingredients they needed to become good students and good people. I raised them to be honest and not deceitful or disrespectful. I wanted to instill in them the truth that this world is not always kind, that they will go through difficult things, and that they will have good days and bad days. And, I tried to help them navigate chaos by being honest and telling the hard truth.

I know all too well that my personality conflicted with Jasmine's, and her shutting me out was her way of coping with a mother who rarely compromised.

By this time, Jacoby had moved out, and I realize that this is a time most teenagers experience puberty; their minds and bodies going through a whirlwind of changes. I expected some change, but not what we got.

Jasmine began distancing herself from us, shutting us out of her everyday life, and not wanting to attend family activities or functions. When we did drag her to places, she sat silently, and never had more than two words to say to anyone. She would answer questions with single word answers, and she never initiated conversations.

We took her to church on Sundays, but she refused to participate in any functions the church sponsored, even for the youth. Later, she revealed she didn't believe in God or Jesus, which shook me for a moment. We had a very limited conversation about what her beliefs were, but she revealed she didn't have any; she just didn't believe in *that*.

The very thought of this troubled both me and my husband, so I began to seek advice from her primary care doctors.

They suggested counseling and possibly medication.

During her high school years, her attitude worsened. I stopped taking her to functions because she would sit on the floor and not say anything to anyone. I continued taking her to church, Sunday after Sunday, in hopes that something she heard would help her to get a better understanding of who God is and what He can do for her. To my dismay, there were no changes.

Our relationship was strained and stressful, at best. She was, in my opinion, selfish, self-centered, and self-absorbed. If our plans had nothing to do with her, she was not interested.

I became convinced she hated her parents. So, we sought counseling services from a few places while she was still a minor, and we even attended a few sessions, but there was no change. A psyche evaluation performed by a licensed psychologist suggested she was slightly depressed.

As time went on, she saw a primary care doctor who prescribed her anti-depression medication, which I believe she still takes today; and truthfully speaking, I didn't see much change.

We tried everything, yet she was determined to give us nothing. Nothing that is, except pure attitude, and any other time, she stayed in her room with her cell phone glued to her hands.

Typical teenage stuff, right?

I was looking forward to her twelfth-grade year; however, it was not at all what I had planned. I could see God lying on his back, laughing so hard, that tears were coming out of His eyes.

During this final year of secondary school, I had to force her to take senior photos. She wanted a class ring but didn't want to go to the ring dance. I took her out to get a prom dress because I believed she was going to the prom. However, she had never told me she had broken up with her "boyfriend," and that she wasn't going to the prom.

Fortunately, I didn't spend a lot of money on the dress, shoes, and accessories. Still, she never stopped me from buying them.

I don't want to get to the end of my chapter and not give you a better understanding of my role in the further breakdown of our relationship. One day, during her early high school years, we got into a physical altercation because of a shirt or "half-shirt" she was wearing to go out with friends. My husband told her to come to me and let me see it. I told her that she needed to put a tank top underneath it, or change it because she couldn't go out of the house wearing it. She was argumentative, and we went back and forth on why I felt it was inappropriate.

Reaching for the bottom of her shirt, I attempted to explain my issue being that it was too short and revealed too much skin.

She knocked my hand away, and I lost my temper and punched her in the face. She swung back, and a fight ensued. My husband had to pull us apart, and I screamed at her to "get out of my house."

Thankfully, she didn't.

When I was finally able to calm down enough, I tried to have a conversation with her. What she said seemed to have turned on the "lightbulb" in my head.

She said, *"A parent should never hit their child."*

Initially, I felt confused because my parents spanked me and my siblings as children as a form of discipline. I asked her, what disciplinary "action" she felt was appropriate. She said she didn't know and that I basically needed to figure it out.

Afterward, however, I felt awful because the physical fight was not a spanking; nor was it a form of discipline. Instead, I had lost control of my emotions and not handled the situation well, and to this day, I regret it. Nevertheless, as bad as I felt about the entire situation, I still had to be her parent and make decisions she may not like.

While I don't think either of our behavior on that day was correct, I was the adult, and I think my inability to handle the situation better, contributed to Jasmine shutting me out almost completely. I am still confused as to why she shut-out her dad.

I could swear I heard God laughing again.

During her senior year in high school, she worked, but we still provided for all of her needs (and most of her wants). Her money was her money; she used it for whatever she wanted. She had access to a car she drove at will, she had the latest iPhone, and she had access to everything we owned.

In my mind, she was simply a spoiled and self-centered brat.

One August day in 2014, my dad passed. We lived in different states, and I had been calling him for about three or four days, but he wasn't returning my calls. I felt horrible because I was visiting my mom and hadn't gotten to see him before I had left town. I asked my mom (they hadn't been a couple for more than 40 years) to go over to his place and find out what was going on.

Anxious and nervous, I didn't have a good feeling about this.

My mom called me in tears, and I was devastated. My dad had died in his apartment, four days prior, alone.

As I type this, I can barely hold it together. The memory of that day still makes me extremely sad. I left work early, and while lying in bed, Jasmine came home. I said to her, "Granddad died today." I think she asked, "Which one?" and I said, "My dad."

Silence.

She never told me how she felt, nor did she ask me how I felt. She simply turned, went into her bedroom, and stayed; completely void of emotion. She didn't seem to mourn his loss or cry one tear.

I was shocked and dumbfounded. This couldn't be the same child who had tried to please everyone, could it?

For her high school graduation, she didn't care who came. She didn't order invitations, announcements, or thank you cards, not even a yearbook; I did all the ordering. I sent out all the announcements, invitations, and thank you cards; however, I made her write them out in her own handwriting.

She didn't care that her paternal grandparents had driven twelve hours to attend her graduation; she didn't spend one hour with them alone. Her grandparents had doted over her since the minute they laid eyes on her, and she had spent every summer at their home, with them showering her with love and attention.

You couldn't ask for better grandparents.

Still, Jasmine was cold and unconcerned about their feelings, and they took notice. I had no idea what to do, or what to say in her defense because she treated us the same way.

Before Jasmine left for college, I wrote her a letter. I wanted to make it clear to her, that no matter what was going on in my life, she would always be a priority... and I wanted her to know I loved her more than life itself.

I want to share it with you:

7/12/17

To my baby girl Jasmine,

Today is your father's and my 20th year anniversary, and you are my inspiration. After reading a letter from another mother, I wanted to tell you the things I've never said to you before.

This is my LOVE letter to you.

Before you were born, I purposely planned your conception. I got off BC so that you could be born. Now it's true, I didn't know whether you would be a girl or a boy and I really didn't care, nor did your dad. We had the name Jasmine or Jalen already picked out. I looked forward to being pregnant, and although we lived in FL during my pregnancy, it wasn't uncomfortably hot. It was very pleasant and peaceful.

You came a week early. You were scheduled to be born Feb 28, 1999; however, during my weekly doctor's visits, my blood pressure was elevated and the doctor didn't want to risk me or you, so that day, I was not able to go home, I had to go directly to the maternity ward where they proceeded to induce labor.

Well, you came sometime after midnight/early morning on Feb 18th. After you were delivered, my full motherly-protective mode kicked in. You see, early in my pregnancy, there was a baby girl in the Jacksonville area who had been kidnapped hours after she was born. So, I was very nervous, and wouldn't have been able to move forward, had anything happened to you. I made your dad follow the nurses and never take his eyes off of you.

SN: That baby today is 18 or 19 years old, and she was found earlier this year, and reunited with her natural family after 18 years of being missing. I saw it on the news.

During delivery, your dad looked at you and announced "it's a boy", followed by the nurse's announcement, "it's a girl". Then, they brought you close to me, and one look and I thought to myself, why is her nose spread across her face like that? It may take a while for her head to grow big enough to support it. But after that, every second, of every minute, of every hour of the day, I couldn't stop thinking about my new baby. I wanted to know what you were doing at all times. And although there were slight complications, and I wasn't able to hold you as much as I liked, you were on my mind constantly.

You grew up so fast, and you were so smart, and you had the same personality you have now; a bit of independence and dependence at the very same time. I kept thinking, my baby is a genius. I remember the stories of you playing, hiding behind the sofa, and sneaking up on me at just 8 months. You had bells on your shoes because you decided you no longer wanted to crawl like normal babies. You wanted to exert your independence by walking at EIGHT months. Who does that?

Thinking about your baby years brings back all kinds of feelings of joy I had. You were such a quiet baby, and full of joy; you loved me and your dad the same amount, you had no favorite... well at that time. Your dad was a hands-on dad. He was with you every moment he could be, he let you play his video games, he let you fall asleep on him, and he let you eat peanuts when you had no teeth to chew them. But that's the type of dad he is. He loves you from the top of your head to the bottom of your feet. We hurt when you hurt, we're sick when you're sick, and we're happiest when you're happy.

There are way too many good times to put into this letter; some you may remember and some you may not. Some we were able to memorialize through pictures and some not. Now that you are 18, and on your way to college, I just wanted you to know a few things. I still think about you every minute of the day and hope you're okay. I hope that you're safe and unharmed and making the right choices. I won't blame you for making mistakes, we all do. The older you get, the more you'll make, and however, the key is to learn from them and not to make the same one twice. My only hope is that something you've learned from your dad and I will help you make the right decisions when times get difficult. You will make mistakes, but what's helpful, is learning from others' mistakes and not repeating them.

There will be times when you grow weary and want to give up, please don't. Never give up, tell yourself "failing is not an option". In the end, you will be glad you didn't. Right now, you think you don't believe in God, but that's because he hasn't revealed himself to you yet. I can only say, one day he will and when he does you will be glad. I'll move on now.

I already notice that you have manners and a good heart, and that you are a very sensitive young lady, and I'm proud of the person you've become. There are two things I think will help you to be successful:

(1) *Success comes from standing out, not fitting in. You don't have to follow the crowd; they don't always know what's ahead of them.*

(2) *And (2) {Good} manners will take you places, money can't, or won't. Always be polite and respectful, even when others are not.*

Well, I'm going to end this letter now. I just want you to know, as long as I'm alive on earth, you will always be my favorite girl, and I will always be here when you need me. You got my number, but just in case you don't, it's easy XXX-XXXX.

Call me; I'm just a phone call away.

Good luck and I wish you much success on your new journey in life.

P.S. I look forward to {using} your new nickname "Dr. Jai"

Love Always,
Mommy

Today, Jacoby is a sergeant in the U.S. Marine Corp, and doing quite well. I couldn't ask for a better son. He's polite, respectful and loves his family. Although I didn't go the "traditional" route, things turned out just fine.

Jasmine is now a freshman in college, and at the time of this book's publishing, she will have completed her first full year. I have noticed, however, a slight change in her attitude towards us, but not much.

My turning point was when I felt defeated, completely unappreciated, and overwhelmed with her attitude.

I decided I had done all I could... the rest was up to her.

I've noticed small improvements, and things appear to be looking up for us. When we talk now, she gives more than just one-word responses to my questions.

She actually initiates conversations, but again, this is rare. She asks us how we're doing, and she asks about her grandmother, my mom who lives with us, and also about Sierra, her dog.

I am hopeful that we can one day have the relationship I've always dreamed about. I look forward to the day when she calls on me for advice, no matter how minuscule.

And, I look forward to sharing moments like college and med school graduations, new engagements, wedding planning, baby planning, and other life's ups and downs.

I'll take it, whatever it is, I will be here waiting to play my role. I also know, our story has not yet made it to the end, there's more to come.

Along the way, I've learned:

1. I had to forgive myself. I had to stop beating myself up for being who God made me to be. We are not all cut from the same cloth, and we do not all have the same experiences.

2. Parenting doesn't come with instructions. Although Dr. Spock will have you believe otherwise, not all kids will fit into a "category."

3. Seek help from professionals, and don't be afraid of medication recommendations; however, do your own research. The internet is a great source for product information. There is a "stigma" within our community that makes us ashamed to seek professional help or advice for fear of looking "cray-cray." Don't fall into this trap.

4. Have patience. Everything has a turning point; nothing stays the same.

5. You won't always make the "right" decision(s). It's hard to know what the right decision is, but follow your instincts, and seek God first. Keep Him at the forefront of your decision-making and when the time comes, He will provide direction.

6. To never give up and never stop trying.

In my small way, I wanted to leave a "legacy," that at any time, my children will be able to pick up and read, and know how much I loved and cared for them; they never have to wonder.

I know my story is not unique, and I know that I'm not alone; others have had, or will have, similar stories.

Finally, when you hear God laughing, don't get upset, just laugh out loud and seek His guidance. He has already provided us with a "guide" we can reference at any time, and please remember, prayer does change things.

If nothing more, praying provides hope, and I have high hopes that things will be better between me and Jasmine.

And then, we can laugh together.

You're my Brother; Not my Son

PATRICE TRICE BROWN

*"Whoever claims to love God yet hates a brother or sister is a
liar. For whoever does not love their brother and sister, whom
they have seen, cannot love God, whom they have not seen."*
~ 1 John 4:20 [NIV]

To My Brother:

How many times have you said to yourself, *I wish I knew
back then what I know now?*

We've all probably said that. The thing that you don't get is,
you would have altered the greatness that you have become. You
would have never made the mistakes, fallen down, picked yourself
up, and made the necessary corrections.

You know there is no such thing as the perfect person right?
We all fall short each and every day of our lives. We strive for

perfection. However, as long as we remember that nothing is impossible for you or me to achieve, we don't need to worry about what we didn't know back then.

If we do the BEST we can, that's what truly matters.

I remember my thirteenth birthday so well. Mom was six months pregnant with you. She got up, got dressed, and walked me to the bus stop. You see, I was about to start high school. She explained she was going to need my help taking care of you. Mom worked all of her life; therefore, I assumed she meant just while she was at work.

So, I asked what do I do?

She explained that I would be helping with the feeding, changing diapers, stuff like that. You have to understand, for me that was strange. You see, all of the girls in the family knew the rules. DO NOT bring a baby into our parents' home! Can you imagine how at thirteen, telling me I would be taking care of a baby was totally crazy; especially, a baby that was not mine!

Three months later, you were here.

Our grandmother told me about this spot on the top of your head. She told me about the thing on your belly; how it would fall off on its own. This was a bit much to digest.

I remember the first time I got to hold you. You were three months old. I was a little scared of you because your head would wobble, you would wiggle, and that was too much for me. I thought I would drop you or something.

Yet, while in my arms, your little hand wrapped around my finger, and you just stared right in my face.

This was the moment I knew I would be your protector. I would protect you from men, women, boys, and girls.

You, my brother, changed the course of my life. You see, I was heading down a path of destruction. I was fighting people on a daily basis. I was fighting with *and for* our cousins. The men in my life wanted me to learn to defend myself, and that I did to the best of my ability. That was all I knew how to do. Be angry and fight.

Now, there was a different type of fight in me. I would fight to make sure you never went through what I was going through. You would feel wanted and loved. You would know that you matter.

Of course, our mother naming you what she did, did not help our situation at all. I'm cracking up as I type this. Parents must think about the names they give their children. These are the names we must carry for the rest of our lives. Still laughing to myself, I thank God that you are six feet four and muscular.

Well, taking care of you went a lot further than changing diapers and the occasional bottle. I was going to school, and rushing straight home to take care of you so our grandmother could go to work. Taking care of you was a family affair. You were a busy little guy; into everything.

If it wasn't nailed down, you were touching it.

One of our Aunts who thought it was a crime that you were in the crib while I cleaned, did homework, and cooked, took you upstairs to her house... you were back downstairs within five minutes.

Never heard about how bad it was for you to be in a crib again.

You went through a grandmother, two aunts, and two male cousins before they all started turning off lights and locking doors when they saw you coming.

The funny thing is, you weren't twelve months old yet. There was no terrible two's; we got the HELP US LORD months! When mom would come home from work, she would complain about the crib prison. She would take you out, play with you for a little while, and then I'd hear your name at the top of her lungs.

Back in the crib prison you went.

If we didn't change you when you were ready to be changed, you would throw the diaper over the crib, or just tear it off where you stood. Again, you were not even a year old.

Everywhere I went, you were right there with me; pushing you around in that stroller, the neighbors thought you were *my* son.

I can remember the first steps you took. You were about ten months old. You never liked being in your walker; you would stand up behind it and push it. So, one day, I decided to move it from in front of you. I stood in front of you and motioned for you to come to me. You wobbled all the way over. I was so excited, I called Cousin S. downstairs, and we did it all over again.

This time, you wobbled over to her. We were both so excited by this that when both of our parents came home, we sat them in the living room, told them to call you, and you wobbled over to them both. Talk about acting like we had just hit the lotto.

Little did I know, teaching you to walk was going to be the one thing I should have minded my business about. You once sat in our grandmother's living room, cracked open about three eggs on her carpet, and proceeded to scramble eggs on her carpet. Thank God our Cousin A. saved you from being on a milk carton.

Yes, my brother, you were a handful.

By the time you were four, going on five, things got a little easier. I would walk you to school and then head back home. In the eighties, three of us cousins decided to go into the military. We wanted to get away from our parents and our home life.

I was truly worried about leaving you here. And, you did not want me to leave you here. You cried so hard that it broke my heart. This phase of my life had to happen. It was like I was leaving my son behind. I came home earlier than the rest of the cousins; heading right back to see you. I tried living with you and mom again. This was not going to work. Our mother had a little spending problem, and when I got home, your school tuition was behind, her rent was behind; both of which damn near emptied my account.

This is why I left the second and final time.

Spending weekends and summers together would have to do. I had a two bedroom apartment and plenty of room, and at one time, I tried asking mom to let you come and live with me; however, she refused. Nevertheless, there came a point when you moved in with me for the first time. I don't remember when exactly. I just know I got the call from mom asking could you stay with me for a little while. I didn't ask any questions; I just said *yes.*

Whatever happened, I didn't care. It gave us time to bond and get to know each other all over again.

You were living with me for about six months when mom came by to say she had moved into her new place and wanted you home. I asked you what you wanted to do, and you said you would go back with her, as long as you could still come to my house on weekends and our usual summers.

I told you that you were always welcome in my home.

Everything seemed to be going pretty well. I got a job working for the police department, mom got a promotion at her job, and you were still in private school and in the seventh grade.

Then the shit hit the fan.

I remember mom and Aunt J. coming by my house; telling me they needed to talk to me about something very important. I could not believe what they were telling me. She needed me to take custody of you because she might be going to jail.

The first question I asked was, *"Where is my brother?"*

Once she said you were home and fine, all was well with me.

Next, I needed to know what she did and why. As I've told you, mom has a problem with money. She likes having it and spending it; however, she doesn't pay her bills. Well, this great job she had, the promotion she received, and all of the bosses that loved her, found out she was embezzling from the company.

Understand me, I didn't have any feelings for mom. I felt nothing as she told me about what was going on with her. While I had her talking, I asked her about the time you came to live with me for half a year. She explained she was getting evicted and didn't want you to know about it. The charges she was facing, she didn't want you to know about that either.

I'm staring at the woman who gave birth to me, the woman who told me not to lie, cheat, or steal, and she's about to go down for the very things she told me not to do.

We didn't use PC's then. So, I whipped out my typewriter and typed up the paper for mom to sign and have notarized; giving me the right to make all decisions concerning your wellbeing.

When you came to live with me this time, you were different. I felt it in my bones. You needed stability and direction. That's what I got from you the first night you stayed with me. I went to my Sgt. to find out if I could switch to a midnight tour. It took about a week, but it happened. Then I had to come up to your school and make sure the paperwork now said to contact me. It was a good thing that I came to all of your PTA meetings. Your Principal made the transition so easy.

What I didn't know was how much your grades had slipped. However, we got that back on track. Do you remember for your eighth-grade graduation, they created a special award just for you? I still feel that sense of pride when I think about that.

On the way home from graduation, we discussed your continuing with private school through high school.

That summer, mom came back around. She let me know that she would not have to go to jail, that she would be on probation for a few years, and that she was moving to Starrett City and wanted you to come live with her there.

Again, this decision would be totally up to you.

There's a bond between a mother and her son that you don't want to mess with. You love mom, and that is something I never wanted to come between. When you decided you wanted to go and live with her again, it was hard for me but, I had to let the decision stand.

Two years went by with us doing the same as we have done before... weekends and summers. Here we go again! Mom didn't handle her business with the rent again. Like the movie with Sidney Poitier, "Guess Who's Coming To Dinner," *guess who's coming back to live with his sister?*

We did this so often that I lost count.

Nevertheless, you were always welcomed back in with open arms and a refrigerator full of food (laughing). This time, you took me to a place I never thought I would ever be with you. This was the start of the pants hanging off the ass; listening to this new wave of rap music that seems to have made you young brothers lose your minds.

After a car accident, I had to have surgery on my leg. You decided to bring home a report card that looked like it came from Dunkin Donuts with all of those D's on it; walking past me singing Biggie Smalls. When I asked you to knock it off, and you gave me attitude... dear brother, you were about to make me move some furniture up in the place.

When I told you to be quiet and sit down, you would start singing louder! I forgot all about my crutches.

I remember jumping up and thinking, *knock him out!* After everything we've been through, you're gonna disrespect me?

That was the first time I kicked you out of my house. And, you did what I thought you would do. You went to mom's house.

Now, of course, I understand why you went there. You needed a place to stay. You just ticked off the one person who always had your back.

As time went by, I realized you were going stay there. Maybe you had more freedom there to do what you wanted because she felt guilty. I remember calling you to tell you that you should leave half of your stuff with me, just in case mom decided not to pay rent again. As I explained to you, it's easier to replace half than it is to replace all. Again, with this new-found attitude that you're a teenager and a junior in high school, you gave me HELL!

You have never seen the side of me that you encountered after that phone conversation. In those days, I could cut a person off without hesitation. I felt I had done enough for you. I protected you when you were younger and took beatings for things that you did. I had my little after school job and would buy for you before I bought myself anything.

We used to have brother and sister date night at your favorite Chinese restaurant, and now you wanted to give me your behind to kiss because you were 'smelling' yourself?

Now you would meet the person that your mother helped create. I couldn't understand this transformation that had taken place with you so fast. Until I went into the room you used to stay in; finding some weed and cigars. That's when the lights came on in Brooklyn. I guess you forgot what I did for a living.

After further investigation, I found out you were drinking, smoking, and becoming this bully. Some people can smoke the stuff and just get the munchies. Some people smoke it and become quiet. Hell, I tried it and laughed myself to sleep. You, *on the other hand,* became this unlikable person.

You lost your high school sweetheart because of it. You lost close friends because of it. The first time I received a call from the police telling me you were locked up, my heart sank. It was a misdemeanor, but you were arrested, nonetheless.

Between your weed smoking and drinking, you were a young man I no longer wanted to be around.

So, I did what most siblings would do in this situation... I lived my life. My attitude was, you'd come around once you hit rock bottom. You would have to make the determination that you needed help and seek it. Birthdays went by, holidays would go by, and no one knew where you, or mom, were.

And then, out of nowhere, I get a call that mom was evicted again, and you two were now living in Bed-Stuy.

As I said, you made your decision, and I had to respect it no matter what. I didn't know much about God back then, except what I heard; that He is a God of judgment, and we were all going to hell. Thanks to our grandmother, I did know how to pray. I would always pray for you.

I heard you guys were homeless. That bothered me.

How can they be homeless with family right here?

Of course, as soon as I said it, I knew the answer. The family was just tired of it, and mom had burned too many people already. She wasn't on drugs, she wasn't selling her body, and she wasn't mentally ill (or was she?). Yet, she could not stop spending money that she didn't have.

There are families that never come together again until it's too late. Someone has to break the cycle of anger and resentment; that bitterness that most can't let go of. I decided that change would start with me, so, I simply prayed for you and mom, and asked God for a sign to let me know you were okay.

As always, I tried to spend every holiday visiting with our grandmother. This particular Memorial Day in 2007, something was strange; it felt like a change was about to happen. I couldn't put my finger on it, but I knew something was different. The bell rang while we were eating, I got up to answer it, and it was you. You looked so beaten, so tired. You were looking for mom.

That gave me chills.

How could you be looking for mom, if you two are together?

When you said that she was staying with a lady she knew from church and that you were sleeping in the park, anger welled up inside of me; but I knew I had to hold that in. *If your child doesn't have a roof over their head, then neither should you.* Especially, if you're the reason the child has no roof over their head.

I asked you, *"When was the last time you saw her?"* You told me a few days ago. This was the change that was going to take place. This was that strange thing I couldn't put my finger on. I sent you into the bathroom to clean up, and then we sat down and ate food together.

When our grandmother asked me are you two going home, I knew you would be going home with me. This time would be the last time you would not have an address. You are not my son; you are my brother. Still, I basically raised you like my son.

I am now going to drop my guard and make sure you're alright. Like a parent, I had to set up some rules. You are going to get some form of counseling.

The question you asked next answered so many questions I had about you. You asked, *"Why did you keep letting me go back to mom?"* Right then, I imagined what you must have been going through; wanting your mother in your life, but not wanting to live with her, and never wanting to say *no* to her, when she asked you to come back and live with her. You love your mother; there's nothing wrong with that.

I thought what I was doing was the right thing. If at any point, you had said *"No, I want to stay with my sister,"* that would have been the end of that. I would have gone to any court to fight for you. But, that's not what happened. I thought giving you the freedom to make your own choice would be better for you. I never wanted to hear the words, "You kept me from my mother."

Let me explain something to you. Our mother made a lot of mistakes with us; however, I truly believe she loves us. Understand this; she is your mother. I am your sister. She gave birth to us both. How can I tell her she can't have her son back? At the time, I thought I was making the best decision I could make when it came to you two. If we could go back in time and make better decisions, I'm sure both of us would make better ones.

That cannot happen.

I believe everything you and I have been through is for a reason. When you were younger, I would tell you to think twice and move once.

I practice what I teach.

I thought long and hard each time mom came back for you. Each time, I did what I thought was best. This time, you are free dear brother. You don't have to make any decisions.

The decision was made for us.

Now, you are almost thirty-nine years old. You have a good job, and some college under your belt. If the things done to you in your past have not broken you, they have made you stronger and more determined.

Your future is too bright to look back now.

Mom is also doing well. She no longer has that money problem, and we speak daily. I'm thankful for that.

As for me, I am determined to live the abundant life promised. I will forgive anyone because I want to be forgiven. My legacy will not be that Patrice was a bitter, angry, and non-forgiving person. Instead, it will be that she touched the lives of every person she met, loving to support and help others, and making you laugh in the worst of times; you are in a no judgment zone when you're with her. Her motto was *if a person wants to live in your past, let 'em.*

I know what most people think of on Memorial Day; I will always remember it as the day my brother came home.

The day my legacy became #Unchained

I Chose My Own Happiness

DAVINA JENNILE

*"Today I choose life. Every morning when I wake up
I can choose joy, happiness, negativity, pain... To feel
the freedom that comes from being able to continue
to make mistakes and choices - today I choose to feel
life, not to deny my humanity but embrace it."*
~ Kevyn Aucoin

They say some events impact your life so much that they become vivid; you can hear, feel, and taste them as they are permanently imprinted into your memory.

I will never forget the purple and pink Picasso-colored sunset in Aruba that veteran's week. It was my third day in Aruba with my boyfriend, and we had gone for a walk around the private beach attached to our villa. Jason and I were standing on the jagged rock infused sand, with a faint smell of salt water in the air. I was discussing my plans to leave my corporate job when we returned to Georgia.

Dead silence.

Turning around to find out what was wrong, I saw Jason holding a ring in his hand. He looked at me, cleared his throat, and stuttered, "Will you marry me?"

Staring at him and the antique jeweled ring, I nervously replied back with a "Sure! I will marry you."

I spent the next two weeks in bliss, as I had beat the "old goods" after you are thirty odds, I had constantly seen on social media. Then, I woke up on a Saturday morning, and reality had roundhouse kicked me in the stomach. I became overwhelmed with nausea and sick to my stomach, thinking about becoming one with this person. The two voices in my head had a battle of the dances on what I should do about my engagement situation. *You've only dated this guy for seven months. Why do you want to get married?* I asked myself. *Listen, girl, your stock is going down every year, and he is stable, without children, in ATLANTA!*

SECURE THE TRANSACTION!

I figured I would contact my friends for advice because sometimes these chicks knew better than I. Whenever I talked to a friend, I received both words of encouragement *and* looks telling me not to do it.

Later, in January, we purchased a house; however, something in my heart told me not to put my name on the deed. That would be something that would turn out to be helpful during the split of unwanted assets during divorce proceedings.

Still, I was unsure of what to do in this situation with Jason.

Sure, I liked him, but I wasn't sure if I was *in love* with him. The feeling of being in love was something new and that I had never experienced in life. I could not answer that question before my wedding day. Nevertheless, I shook the thoughts out of my head and settled for simply liking him.

That would be enough.

My Jewish wedding was on a partially cloudy day in Savannah, Georgia. While the makeup artist brushed beautiful strokes of lavender across my eyelids, my friends helped me get into my bridal dress. I looked like royalty, yet reality was hammering at my brain. The battle had resumed, and I asked myself, *are you sure you want to do this?* My thoughts went silent, and before I knew it, I had said "I do" under the Chuppah.

We broke the glass and headed to the reception.

The photographer at my wedding had requested a picture of me and Jason at the front of the southern-style house. As she snapped a few pictures of us, she put down her camera, and with a curled lip blurted out, "Do you guys love each other? What type of marriage are you two going to have if you two touch each other like you are in the church?"

I rolled my eyes, and she gave me one more jab of shade, "I guess children are out of the picture," and snapped one final shot before leaving the venue.

We went to our hotel and hung out with friends until night fell. What should have been an intimate night between two people joined as one, turned into my sitting on the bed scrolling on Facebook, while he and his best friends played spades and got drunk until 4:00 a.m.

I am a believer in one old wives' tale of how you spend your wedding night is how your marriage will develop over time.

I don't know when Jason got in the bed, but we woke up next to each other ready to check out at 11:00 a.m. I said my goodbyes to our friends and family, and we headed back to Atlanta as Mr. and Mrs. Boise; in name only.

For the first three months, things had remained as it was prior to our getting married. We had our good moments; yet, it still felt like two strangers living under the same roof. I started to reflect on my childhood and the vision of marriage I had grown up with.

Although not perfect, my childhood was filled with lots of love between my parents. I never wanted for anything, my parents equally supported each other as a team, and they were each other's backbone. However, when I looked at my marriage, it was a foggy and distorted shadow.

I replayed that image in my head for a few more months, as I had started a new job in a psychiatric hospital, working with children. My new position was emotionally and physically draining. Shifting through treatment plans on these patients made me evaluate my own relationship. I remember a younger patient saying all she wanted was to have a family and be loved. I had her draw it for me, and her idea of love was vibrant and inviting, while mine remained a pale and disenchanting shadow.

That night, I ended up working a double shift and went home the next day at 8:00am. Unable to sleep, I sat down on the couch with my tea, and blurted out, *"I like him, but I'm not in love."*

My heart began to race, and it felt like I couldn't breathe; I was having a panic attack. I ran outside for fresh air to calm myself down. I had finally accepted reality... I was in a loveless marriage. I told myself that, *we are here, and this is my life going forward.*

Now in my thirties, my job had both tested my sanity *and* introduced me to what I would make a career choice as a Behaviorist. I had made up my mind and decided on going back to school to get my graduate degree; figuring that Jason would understand, as he already had his graduate degree.

Later that evening, when Jason had gotten home, I had set the table with some shrimp étouffée, brown rice, and freshly squeezed strawberry juice.

As he ate his meal, I exclaimed, "I figured out what I want to do with my career!" and he just stared at me between bites. Smiling from cheek to cheek, I told him, "I will be going back to school for my graduate degree in Behavior Analysis."

He put his spoon down and asked me, "That's nice, but when are you going to give me a child?"

Slightly shocked by his response, I looked at him; reminding him that we had agreed to not have children for the first two years of our marriage. He nodded his head and said, "Well, I will ALLOW you to go to school."

At that moment, I felt like a child receiving permission from her father to do what she wanted. The thought never crossed my mind as to why he felt it was important to give me permission to go to graduate school, and not a simple gesture of support for pursuing my goals. I applied anyway and started my graduate program the next year.

As they say, what doesn't kill you will make you stronger, and graduate school had me on a tightrope; lingering on mental death and physical exhaustion. I worked and interned six days a week while being in school full-time. At the same time, Jason and I never really had time for each other, except at night during our two-minute nightly conversations. He focused on his financial job and sports, and I focused completely on my career.

By my second semester, we were constantly arguing with each other. Weekly threats of divorce were thrown from each other's mouth. The exchanges always ended with him reminding me that I was selfish, I had changed, and that he was sacrificing himself by allowing me to go back to school.

One day, Jason exploded on me and told me that not only had I changed, but "You've become the typical black independent women. What happened to my sweet Davina? You've been in Atlanta or around those Americanized black American women for too long."

I wondered, how the hell a dude from New England could utter such words, but I told him, "I am still Davina, but I am older, and I know what I want in life." I walked away; questioning who this person was that was living with me in my house?

Stomping up the stairs, I decided to Google his aliases. I clicked on an image in Google from him, and was floored with the website it took me to; a private male-only traveling club for minority men who liked to travel to foreign countries for sex and women, because American women (and especially African

American women) had lost their feminine quality. I had married a guy who used to trick off on prostitutes.

That day, the intimacy between us left the building. Now, I was relieved and thankful that I had gotten tested, and continued to practice safe sex while married.

The next day, I went to my friend's house to have a glass of wine and discuss my situation. A friend of his, who just happened to be there and listening to our conversation, interrupted and told me that one of the main reasons my husband had married me, was due to the fact that I had spent a significant amount of my life living overseas.

"What the hell does that mean?" I proclaimed to his friend.

"He thought that since you grew up overseas, you would be a docile, dormant woman he could mold into the person he wanted; one who followed him at his beck and call."

I just smiled at his friend and thanked him for his information. I knew I needed to get out of this marriage, but I needed to be strategic with how I left, and part of me was afraid of starting over again.

Over the next year, I continued working on finishing graduate school and working. We had officially gone one year without intimacy, and I told him that it was due to my going on a spiritual journey. However, as time passed, I thought we could get counseling and work out our differences and salvage our marriage. But, I was always met with "I'm not paying anybody shit to listen to us when we can fix it ourselves."

One day after work, I was sitting in the kitchen reading emails, and I had received an email from one of my professors, asking if I had thought about going back to school for my doctorate.

"Ugh, yes!" That had always been on my to-do list.

I wasn't sure how Jason would respond to me going back to school again, and so soon; therefore, I decided to ask him about it, in the heat of the moment. His response would truly reveal how he saw me as his wife.

So, after we had breakfast the next day, I asked him how he felt about me going back to school for my doctorate. I never got a chance to finish my whole thought, before he went in for the kill. "I ALLOWED you to go to school and get your master's, and now you want to get your doctorate? What about a family? You need to learn your place and learn to make sacrifices."

"What do you mean by sacrifices?"

He scrunched up his nose, placed his hand on the table, and said, "I mean, as a woman, you need to learn to follow your man and do what I tell you."

I just smirked at him and asked him again for clarification. "Are you telling me that if you got the opportunity to go to graduate school or a new job, that I should follow you, but it is different for me?"

With a stern, straight face, and eyes piercing my skin, I was met with a bold, "YES! As a woman, you must sacrifice your goals and dreams for your man. You don't have to like it, but that is the way things are in a relationship."

I finally understood what he had meant when he said that he had *allowed* me to go to graduate school. At that point, I wasn't even shocked and knew I needed to accept that he saw me not as his wife or a woman, but as a girl he could manipulate to satisfy his own needs.

We remained in a sex-less and emotion-less marriage for two more years. We were not a married couple, but roommates; sleeping in different rooms, at my request. I complained about his snoring, but that was just a lie to not be near him.

The imprint of my ring had all but disappeared, as I had stopped wearing it the same night I figured out that he saw me as nothing more than a child.

The more we inhaled the same air, the more disgusted I became with seeing him; to the point of getting a headache or feeling sick. I learned to put on a mask, and bottle up my true intentions of divorcing him until the time was right.

On the outside, I would smile and laugh; while battling rage and hurt on the inside.

One day, he came to me after he had been drinking, trying to be intimate, and I immediately pulled back. He got upset and started yelling at me, "I am your husband, and we haven't had sex in three fucking years. Can I get something?" He pulled down his pants, and I pushed back; grabbing a flashlight.

"What's that on the dick?" I asked him while twirling the flashlight in my hands. He looked, and then before pulling up his pants and going back to his room, told me that it was a scab from shaving the day before.

For the next eight months, we proceeded as roommates, until he again approached me, in the same manner, trying to be intimate. I got up from the couch and grabbed the same pink flashlight. "You still have that scab. It's been almost a year, and now it's raised." I told him that he should probably see a doctor about that magical scab that won't heal.

He came back a week later, showing me his HIV and STD results. All the results were negative, except one thing was missing. His biopsy results!

The following day, I was off and went to the bathroom sink. I found the results that were missing, and the woman in me became a professional photographer and private eye detective that day. I gathered up enough evidence to make the lowest of attorneys hug me for doing the grunt work.

I kept telling myself that I was ready to go, but I needed to make sure I was completely emotional and financially secured.

It had now turned into four years of us doing nothing more than sharing the same address. I remember our sitting on opposite ends of the couch; watching television. I had come to the point where I had no filter with what would come out of my mouth.

As we were watching a "Cheaters" episode, he told me that he would never lie or cheat on me. I laughed; telling him that he was full of shit if he thought I believed that lie.

He told me it wasn't a lie, and that he was "blindly loyal and faithful" to me. My head twisted with warp speed. "Blindly loyal? Did you just say you are blindly loyal to me?"

Repeating himself, he again told me that he was "blindly loyal to me." I heard those words in slow motion, and I finally snapped; all the emotions I had held onto finally manifesting into full rage.

"Blindly loyal to me? Shut the fuck up! Nobody that paid for pussy from prostitutes before we were married knows anything about being blindly loyal. Someone that hides his STD medicine under the sink is not blindly loyal to anyone. We haven't had sex in four years. I am not stupid, and no man is going to go that long without sex, so who the fuck did you fuck?"

I was completely out of character after getting that off my chest. I was in a fight stance and ready to pounce at any moment. He stood up, told me that he did not have any STD and that it was just a scab. He was willing to go to any place to get another test done. I was so angry with the blatant lies that my hands started shaking, and I lunged at him.

He took off toward his room and didn't come out, until later that night when he approached me and assured me that he would get tested again. I declined the offer, told him to go back to the same person who had done his original biopsy and then bring the sealed result to me. Nervously, he told me that he would, and walked back up the stairs to go to bed.

After work the next day, he handed me a sealed envelope from his doctor. I opened it, while he sat on the couch sweating. I knew exactly what it meant having worked in a hospital, but I pulled out my phone and showed him.

At first, he acted confused; telling me that he didn't understand how he had an STD. I sat there smiling and told him to cut the bullshit. "You knew you had an STD from the start, so stop lying to me NOW." He put his head down on his lap and told me that he knew, but was embarrassed to tell me.

My smile widened, and I told him that it wasn't just embarrassing, but the highest level of disrespect to me as a human being. "We got tested before we got married, and during our marriage. What if I would have had sex with you and caught something? You could have put my life in danger."

He apologized and told me he wanted to stay married, but understood if I wanted to leave him. I just smiled and walked away from him. I wasn't upset about the situation, but I hate liars. I not only accepted that I needed to leave, but finally faced the reality of my situation. I had officially checked out of my marriage that day, and there was no turning back.

Immediately, I began looking for places around Atlanta to live, and look for a higher paying job; focusing completely on myself and my well-being. While in the process of transition out of my marriage, I met new people, and one introduced me to non-tactical weapons for women.

Jason saw my weapons and came back two days later with his own stun gun.

I said that was nice, as I charged mine.

Five minutes later, he came back downstairs with a standard gun in his hand and pointed it at my chest. I had become so withdrawn from the relationship that I just stared at him unmoved. I told him, "If you are going to shoot me, then just do it!" He told me to "shut the fuck up," called me crazy, and then told me that he was just joking with me.

After this, I got in my car, and I cried.

Not out of fear, but due to the fact that I had reached a point beyond hating Jason. I didn't need a strategy anymore; I needed to leave before I ended up on the news. At that moment, I made the decision to walk away, and by choosing freedom and being true to myself, it was easy.

Don't let thoughts that you must have a well-thought-out plan, be perfect, or accept things as they are, keep you from being authentic to yourself and your dreams.

When you are ready to chase your own happiness, look at these tips to help you on your journey:

1. **Start Living Now**: Wanting to be perfect is often a problem of putting too much emphasis on the things we cannot control or change. Sometimes, they are so far in the future that we cannot determine the outcome. We fill our minds with ideas of *maybe we are not talented or good enough*. Just stop! No more thinking these thoughts and learn to live in the NOW.

2. **Prioritize Yourself and Choose Happiness:** We are human, and life isn't always full of blissful moments. Even with those less blissful moments, never fall victim to the selfishness of others. Live for yourself and choose happiness.

3. **Follow your Intuition:** That little voice that quietly whispers to us when something does feel right is our inner *self* trying to guide us to the right path. Learn to go beyond just listening; actually, start trusting it.

Following your intuition will save you a lot of time and headache in relationships.

4. **Get a Break out of Prison Card:** When it gets to the point that every morning, night, or second, you are thinking about how great it would be if you could just get out of a particular situation, it's time to release *yourself* from imprisonment. The only person keeping "you" in prison is YOU!

5. **Bring on the New Change in your Life:** Change can be exciting! You don't know what will happen if you leave. It might be bad; it might be good in other ways. You keep putting it off for so long because you're trying to avoid experiencing the unknown. We cannot look into the future and know what our life outcome will be from a life-changing decision. Even if we don't know what life holds for us, it won't hurt to actually try a change.

6. **Stop wondering about the "ifs" and "right":** If you are right for them, then you will be right for them. Many times, we are so caught up in finding the answer to this question that we stop focusing on ourselves. The honest answer to that question is, "possibly, but what about yourself?" Instead of asking if "you" are right for them, ask yourself if "they" are right for you?

7. **Be a Dream and Goal Chaser:** Learn to work hard, and work smart to build your empire; however, never sacrifice yourself in the process. When someone tells you that you cannot do something, keep doing it. If a person cannot support your desires, smile and keep it moving. Don't allow yourself to look back twenty years from now, and tell yourself that you wished you had done something that was important to your dreams and goals.

8. **Don't settle:** Sometimes, we need to stop listening to society's norms or standards. Refuse to settle for being in a relationship that lowers your standards and is loveless. At times, the place we have become accustomed to isn't the where we belong. It is not your home!

We all want to be *happy*, but in reality, we don't always start off on the right path. Sometimes, we are lost in what we want and need in life. The process of finding my inner self, and not settling for what others wanted for me, was an unchaining experience. I think back to who I could have been, had I not given up on myself and my dreams. I am happy that I decided to seek freedom.

My legacy belongs to me and only me. I refuse to be chained and bound by people, with their own desires cast on me.

I *choose* to nurture and love *myself*, to take care of my inner *happiness*, and to never settle for dark holes of nothingness. I encourage you to never give up on yourself!

Finding happiness doesn't come with a map or a *how-to guide*. Instead, it is a thrilling and emotional journey that will develop along the way. When times become so hard that you want to let go or quit, remember my story, and let it be an affirming light in the times of darkness.

I have been in your shoes!

If there is anything I want you to take away from my testimony, it is that you deserve the freedom of your OWN happiness.

Never give up and never settle!

Be Bold. Be You. Be Free. And, Be Happy!

My Legacy is You!

SANDRA DE GREENE

"See that you do not despise one of these little ones.
For I tell you that their angels in heaven always see
the face of my Father in heaven."
~Mathew 18:10 (NIV)

From a very young age, I always pictured you as my daughter. I believe there was a man in the picture, but his image was always obscure and not really that important. He had one job... to give me a baby girl. In my youth, I did not know the particulars of how that could happen; I only knew a man was necessary.

However, it was just going to be me and 'my girl' against the world. We were going to be very close and have dinner together every night. We would have a special time every morning before the day began, or every evening before bed. I would have a cup of coffee or hot tea, and you would have milk or hot chocolate, and we would talk about any and everything. You were going to be able to ask me anything, and I would give you honest answers.

Daily, I would tell you how beautiful and intelligent you were, and you would grow up confident and sure of yourself; prepared for the real world and knowing your options.

I think back and wonder *what in the world made me picture a life as a single mom?*

Years later, while in the military, and following several unsuccessful attempts, I was finally going to have a baby.

There are no words to describe the excitement and joy I felt. When I went for the ultrasound to "confirm" the sex, I was simply going to confirm what I already knew. I was lying there, and the doctor asked me what I wanted. With a huge smile, I said, "A girl." That fathead doctor turned to me and said I should be happy just to have a healthy baby.

My heart dropped. I cried all the way home.

Your grandmother called later that evening to see what the doctor had revealed. She thought it was so funny. She asked what I was going to name him, and I said, "Boy." She replied, "So, you're Jane, and the daddy is Tarzan?"

I had absolutely no boy names picked out because I knew my God was going to give me my heart's desire.

I went through the rest of the pregnancy with a sort of diminished excitement. I had no idea what I was going to do with a boy-child. Nevertheless, when the nurse placed you in my arms, I took one look at you and became overcome with a love and joy that filled my heart.

My first thought was, *I love you so much, but I can't take you out in public.* You looked rough! You were mine, and I loved you dearly, yet I knew how people could be; I was not going to have people talking about my baby. You looked like a cross between a sumo wrestler and something I cannot describe.

No one would believe how awful you came out looking; however, we have actual evidence.

As soon as you were born, they had cleaned you off and took a picture. It did not even capture all the ugly. Your grandmother still has that awful picture. I definitely did not want it.

Then, each day you began to look better and better. Believe me when I say, you could not have gotten worse. By the time I took you home, after an extended stay due to complications, I felt it safe to take you out in public. You had become adorable and cute. I used to get mad at people for thinking you were a girl. How could they think you were a girl when you were wearing boy's clothes?

This happened for years!

You would think the fact that I wanted a little girl would make me happy that you were as cute as one, but *hell no*. The first several months of your life were rough for me. You had many issues. What with the club feet, lack of weight gain, and feeding issues, I was at my wit's end. I had no clue what I was doing, and I felt so helpless and alone. I thought it would be better for us if I was with my family in the States.

So, I left Germany and went back home with you in tow.

Worst decision I ever made in our life. I should have stayed in the military where I at least had a steady income and a place to live. I never felt like I had come home. Instead, I felt like a stranger visiting a foreign land; living with different family members. It would take some time before we would have a place to call home.

After seeing several doctors, I discovered that you were developmentally delayed. Yes, I had to be told this because I did not know enough about children and milestones to know that you were not doing the things normal babies did at the same age. I felt like crap and a poor excuse for a mom, but it is what it is.

Now we knew what was wrong, which lead to more doctors and included therapy several times a week. Then, we found an early developmental day program for you that you attended five days a week for a couple of hours a day.

Everything seemed fine for a while. You seemed happy, and I was just going through the motions, until the day the teacher called and told me that when you came to school, you cried all day and they had no idea what was wrong. I was flabbergasted. You were always in a great mood when you left and always in a great mood when you came home.

The next day, I put you on the bus for school as usual. After you left, I got dressed and went up to the school. I could hear you crying as soon as I came in the door. As soon as you saw me, you immediately stopped crying; crawling over to me so that I could pick you up.

You were my happy baby again.

In sitting down with the teacher, I learned that you would start crying as soon as you got close to the school and that you would get happy again as soon as you turned onto our block to come home. The teacher realized that you were crying because you missed me.

There were times when you would crawl out of the room I was in, to go to another room, and as soon as you got there, you would start crying. Of course, I would go and pick you up and bring you back into the room I was in.

I didn't think anything of it, because, to me, you were a baby... and geesh, that's what babies did. They cried.

I have to admit, when we figured out that the problem was you're missing me, it kind of made my day. For so long, I believed that I was not that important to you. That you not only did not know who I was to you, but you did not really even care. I did not believe it was your fault. I just believed that was the nature of your handicap. Previously, there had been numerous times when I tried to hug or kiss you, that you would push me away. It happened so frequently that subconsciously I think I distanced myself from you, in an effort to keep my feelings from being hurt.

Now, I knew you recognized that I was someone important in your life, and that made me feel amazing.

When I would take you to your grandmother's for a couple of days, I would not sneak out of the house. I would purposely say *goodbye* to you, knowing that you were going to cry. My mom would get mad, but I was thrilled. Yes, it was an awful thing to do, but I loved knowing that you did not want me to leave you.

This reminds me of when you were only one year old, and you realized that if you put your arms up, I would pick you up.

My brother told me that I shouldn't pick you up every time you wanted me to. I told him that I was basically trying to reinforce your understanding and communicating your need. However, if I am really honest, it made me feel as if you wanted me to hold you. That is the real reason why every single time you put your arms up to me, you were picked up by me.

Several years passed, and finally, we had our own place.

Just you and me.

We had a routine. You attended school during the day, and I was home every day to take you off the bus. I tried working several different times; unfortunately, you began having febrile seizures. Those types of seizures come with illness. So, every time you had a cold, and it brought on a fever, you would have seizures. Also, those illnesses would never last merely one or two days; they would last at least a week or more causing me to have to leave a job. Finally, I gave up on working for a while.

I did manage to get my associate's degree during that time; able to go while you were in school. However, there were a few classes I was unable to physically attend; classes I knew were a conflict with your schedule. For those, I would speak to the professor in the beginning and get the okay to be a 'no-show' and I basically just showed up to take exams.

My schooling was a challenge. However, it was also the happiest time for me. I loved going to school. I loved being just Sandra. I was not a mom, not a daughter, not a sister; I was just Sandra and happy as hell competing with other students for the best grades.

Wow. I miss that time.

It is not that I did not love you Pooh, but everyone needs a break from their life once in a while. I know I did not always take you out with me, but it was not because I was ashamed or embarrassed by you. It was because I could not stand how some people reacted to you. Although I get that most people are not used to being around the handicapped, it was still annoying.

Sometimes I thought it best to not bring you into a situation where I might be tempted to punch someone in the face; therefore, it was more about keeping me out of jail, not hiding you.

I think I was kind of afraid of you until you were about seven or eight. You would get upset and not eat your food. I was constantly afraid of upsetting you. You were driving the bus, and I was your passenger sitting in the back seat until my stop came up or you needed something. One day, I got enough balls to put my foot down. You had never liked touching food. I had to put it in your mouth with my fingers or on a spoon. If I put it in your hand, you immediately dropped it on to the floor.

For about a week, twice a day, we would work on you handling food. I especially used sticky food. That was absolutely the worst for you. I made sure it was something sweet-tasting though.

I would guide your hand to it, help you pick it up, and keep your fingers closed so you could not drop it back down. Then, I would guide your hand to your mouth until you closed your lips around it. You always enjoyed the sweet, but you still fought every step of the way. Finally, you would hold your own food in your hands.

There were many times when I thought you would have been better off with someone else. Yet, here I was teaching you something.

Yes!

I remember when I taught you how to kiss. Then, one day you were doing something you were not supposed to do, and I yelled, "come here!" You kindly crawled over to me, stood up, kissed me on the lips and crawled away. It felt as if you had patted me on the head and said, *you will be alright now*.

I still laugh when I think about how you always felt a kiss made everything alright... and you were right.

Your kisses always made everything better.

The hardest thing to teach you was how to use the toilet. By this time, I was working, and you had to have been around fourteen or fifteen years old; your behind was way too big for a potty. It was easy to deal with diapers in the house, but out in public with your big butt, not so much. I had no idea where to start; however, necessity is not only the mother of invention, it is also the mother of frustration and inconvenience.

We would stay in the bathroom until you made some magic. At night, I would get up every two hours, wake you up, and put you on the toilet. Needless to say, I was a walking zombie at work. I don't remember how many weeks it took. But, I do remember being surprised when I got up out of bed to go wake you and found you sitting on the toilet.

Oh my goodness! You were the best baby in the world.

I still thought of you as *my baby*, and I was going to finally get a good night's sleep. It is even hard to remember those sleep deprived nights, but you did it!

I was beyond proud of you.

Do you recall when you were really little, and you discovered biting? I couldn't get you to stop, no matter what I tried. My brother would laugh every time you bit him, and as a result, you thought it was a fun game. I even tried pinching you. Nothing worked. Then, one day you bit me especially hard, I literally saw stars. When I came back to myself, and I could focus and think again, I bit your fathead back.

I don't care who is judging me right now because your little fathead never bit anyone ever again. I cannot stop laughing as I recollect that time. We had our fair share of great moments like these, and I reveled in every one of them.

Still, you were seven years old when I realized I had never told you that I loved you. I had not grown up in an affectionate household, yet that should not mean that you did not deserve affection. I tried to say it for a while and then I reverted to my old ways. I told myself that you didn't understand the words anyway.

That does not make it right. It is just an excuse.

I hope, even though you may not understand the words that you at least feel my love for you. Even though you may not be able to explain the feeling, I am hopeful that you recognize it. That is one of the reasons why I make you give me a hug every day when I get home.

Occasionally, I have thought about how different my life would have been without a handicapped child. Sadly, there have been many times that I regretted having you. I used to think that I would give you up without issue. Then, you would face a medical situation, and I would fall apart at the thought of losing you. It seemed as if each time I arrived at that 'woe is me' place, we would face a life-threatening issue, and I would be reminded that you not only need me, but I needed you too.

Look at God work.

Yes, the first couple of seizures freaked me out and had me scared out of my mind. However, after years of it happening over and over again, I had to get a grip. I had to get extremely dispassionate because I could not afford to fall apart every time something happened. Not to mention, after a while, it just became part of our life. Know that my calmness during the bad times was not because I did not care, but because I could not let the situation overwhelm me and then not be in the right frame of mind to do what needed to be done.

I did so much wrong. It was difficult to hear your baby has multiple handicaps, is severely retarded, and orthopedically impaired with autism. As old as you are now, I still find it difficult to talk to people about your issues. It still hurts to say it out loud. I know there is a little distance between us. It is because I was always worried that one day there would be an issue that we would not get through and that you would be taken from me. I knew that would destroy me. I had to be prepared to go on without you. Thank God that day has never come and I am sorry for keeping pieces of myself from you.

For years, I wondered why me? I never understood why I was the one chosen to have a severely handicapped child. I was not equipped for it. I was not the best person for you to be with. The funny thing is, as hard as it has been for both of us, I am glad you are a boy. I know for a fact that I would not have been able to deal with a severely handicapped little girl.

I guess God did know what He was doing.

Fortunately, many years ago, I got ahold of a book that basically helped me to accept the fact that there will be things we might never understand. I was finally able to stop saying, *why me*, and just accept you for who you are.

I don't know what may happen to you if I leave this earth before you. Who will take care of you? What if someone does something wrong to you and I am not here to kick butt? How can I protect you if I am not here?

These thoughts terrify me.

Nevertheless, I fully believe in the Lord, and I know if He allowed you to be born He will provide a way for you to be taken care of. I trust that if you do not leave this world with me, you will still be in His arms.

Raising you was difficult, but you are the best of me.

Because you are my only child. You are my only son. You are my legacy.

My legacy is you!

Reclaiming My Happily Ever After

MAYA LYNN

*"Happily Ever After
is not a fairy tale; it's a choice."*
~ Fawn Weaver

Once upon a time, there lived a fabulous princess from a small kingdom in the land of Windsor. This princess lived in a beautiful white castle atop a rolling hill. She was deeply loved by her parents, the King and Queen of Windsor. And, she was adored by her brother, the prince.

Her life was the stuff that dreams were made of.

So, maybe I'm exaggerating... *a little.* I'm no Disney princess, but my childhood definitely seemed like it was right out of a storybook, or at least, an 80's family sitcom.

I grew up in a suburb of Hartford, Connecticut. Windsor, a culturally diverse middle-income community, was the idyllic setting of my seemingly perfect life. I literally lived in a white house on a hill, on a little more than a quarter of an acre of green. My backyard had a swing set, an apple tree, and a patio that my father built.

It was truly blissful.

But, while the Windsor estate was my family's home for almost 40 years, our fairy tale didn't begin there. It actually began in Long Island, New York. My parents, Carl and Dorothy, met in a little town of Riverhead, a town that, to this day, is about 93 percent related to me. My father was the star quarterback of the Riverhead High School Football team, and my mother was a slim, quirky beauty who enjoyed drama club.

After high school, my father served in the military and attended Syracuse University, while my mother went to St. Mary's, a nursing school in New York. Yet, they never forgot about each other, returning to Riverhead to marry in 1967. They moved to Hartford in 1970, when my father was offered a job with the Urban League. He had a choice: Hawaii or Connecticut.

He chose Connecticut in order to stay close to family.

In January 1971, they had my brother Jason, the prince, and 3 1/2 years later, they had Princess Maya (that would be me).

We lived in a little, brown Cape Cod in Bloomfield, CT where all of the neighbors knew each other and the entire neighborhood co-owned a dog named Charlie. After a few years, we needed more space, so we moved to Windsor, where we lived until 2017. For almost 40 years, the Harris family lived in that white house on the hill with our dogs, Freckles, Coco, and Buffy, and a few geriatric gerbils, Maymay, Yogi, Boo-Boo, and Ms. Pacman.

We should have had our own reality show.

Not only did I have a textbook-perfect living environment, but my circle of friends came straight from a Benetton ad. First, there was Mindy, a shy yet funny Filipina who lived down the street. Mindy and I started kindergarten together and had the same classes for seven years. Most Saturdays, I would wake up, and Mindy would already be in my kitchen - I think she had a key.

Alicia, a no-holds-barred Jamaican-American lived a few blocks away. She and I were mortal enemies throughout kindergarten with Mindy stuck in between. However, she became one of my closest friends and someone you could always count on if the sh*t hit the fan.

Mandy, a curly-haired Polish-American, was added to the crew in middle school. She and Alisha were practically twins if you did not take their race into consideration. Tanae, a track star whose family was from St. Kitts, also joined the crew in middle school due to her immense flute playing talent (actually none of us were really good, but we enjoyed being band geeks). Then there was Cindy, who is now a high-powered attorney, whom I had more life-endangering adventures with than we care to recall. I'm not sure what Cindy's heritage is, but my brother always just called her White Maya. Peg, my twin flame from middle school, was Japanese.

And well, there was just a host of other girlfriends from so many places, my mother called us the 'little UN'; school was our meeting ground.

I stayed busy! I was Ms. Extracurricular and a great student - chatty, but smart and active in all kinds of school clubs. We attended church every Sunday morning, afternoon, Tuesday and Wednesday evening, and most Saturdays. I pretended to do field events on the track team. I went to Girls' State. I sang in the choir. I was a church usher, and I competed in oratorical contests.

All of these activities led to my graduation from high school with a full academic scholarship to Virginia Union University in Richmond, VA. My church gave me a Bible and a book scholarship. The Junior League gave me $500.

My family, church, and community were proud!

I mean, we weren't the Huxtables, but we were pretty damn close. So, how did I end up, at age 21, a single mother on welfare?

What went wrong?

Easily, I can give you a laundry list of excuses. I can point fingers. I can blame others. However, I'm sure you would see right through all of that, so I won't waste your time.

I simply messed up. I ignored my parents' rules and made mistakes. And I made more mistakes trying to clean up the other mistakes. I hurt good people. I became selfish. And I lied. Why? Wasn't I the girl with the fairy tale childhood? What made me want to put any of that in jeopardy?

ENVY.

My freshman year at Virginia Union was eye-opening. Away from my parents for the first time in my life, I found myself living in a building with all girls, making decisions on our own, with minimal adult input. I found myself around young women who had not grown up with the rules I had to adhere to, and I was envious. They were so free. They wore high heels and makeup and cursed openly. They played spades and drank and wore short skirts and low-cut tops. They had gold chains and big earrings.

It seemed that EVERYONE was from Brooklyn and personally knew Biggie (a few actually did). They had jewel-colored pagers and CD players. They were, in every way, cooler than me and I wanted in. They were surrounded by boys, partying, driving fancy cars, and wearing the best clothes. They seemed to have it all, and I was just a church girl from Connecticut.

It was the perception of their lives that earned my respect. Still, I didn't recognize that their lives were just as difficult as mine. In fact, they were significantly more difficult.

Yet, it didn't matter.

All of those things began to make my fairytale seem like a nightmare that I no longer wanted to be a part of.

I tried to emulate what I saw. My clothes got tighter and shorter. I got the newest hairstyle. I bought the big earrings and make-up. I wanted to erase the princess. My circle of friends, who had equally idyllic upbringings, all attempted to do the same things. We wanted to fit in. We needed to be admired. And we were... maybe a bit too much.

The college boys began to take notice, and we were unafraid to flaunt it. I was even more determined, at any cost, to leave my past behind. While my grades remained high, as I couldn't risk losing my scholarship, I had sunk to my lowest.

While my days were filled with academic discourse, my nights were spent drinking, smoking, and sleeping with whomever I chose. I felt free. I felt grown. I had finally "escaped" my fairy tale.

Then, reality caught up with me. On the eve of my graduation from college, with a promising career in front of me, I found out that I was pregnant. It was a nightmare. All of a sudden, my fairy tale came screaming back at me. The perfect childhood I had experienced, and the reputation of my family was in jeopardy because of my actions.

Still, even in this life-halting moment, I thought I could take the easy way out. I even considered abortion. Until I had a dream.

One night, I dreamed about two small boys playing soccer outside of the veterinary office in Windsor. Now that's not the typical place where kids play soccer but, there they were. Two small kids were laughing it up, enjoying life, with me standing on the sideline, smiling them on.

When I woke up, I quickly realized that all of the excuses I was making were selfish. What did I have in front of me? Well, I wasn't married, but I most certainly had a college degree in my hand. Although I would have to postpone working, I had a teaching certificate. I would soon have a job with full benefits.

I thought about the countless women who struggled to raise their kids, yet managed to survive and become successful.

It led me to believe that I could do the same, especially with so many advantages. So, I decided to do the right thing for me and become a mother.

It was the best decision I had ever made because a month later, I found out that not only was I going to be a mother, but I was going to be a mother of twins!

While I was excited about the blessing I was being given, I also realized that I was completely unprepared to be a parent of two! It was time to do that one thing I'd been avoiding.

I called home.

After letting my mother know what was going on, I was surprised that she already knew something was wrong; actually expressing relief when I broke the news. "Maya, I thought you were on drugs! You've been acting so strange lately; I've been trying to figure out if we were going to be able to afford rehab for you! But, a baby? We can handle a baby! In fact, we can handle two!"

Then she said, "But, honey, you are going to have to tell your father yourself."

I immediately broke down. The one person I was afraid to disappoint above anyone else was my father.

I'm definitely a daddy's girl. Even when my mother became a Jehovah's Witness and my brother went off to college and stopped going to church, I was dad's road dog. I tried to join as many church groups as possible. I wanted him to be proud of me and everything I did. So, sharing this news with him... well, I knew it would break his heart.

"Dad I need to tell you something. I've already spoken with Mom about this but, it's important that I speak to you too."

There was silence on the phone as I told him everything. He waited a moment and said, "OK, here's your mother." That was it, but I knew what that meant. He had nothing to say.

Two weeks later, I received a letter from him in the mail. He expressed his disappointment in me. He couldn't understand how

I managed to go off to college and excel, then do something so foolish. He told me he was afraid that I would just become another statistic. You see, my father worked for the Federal government in the Department of Housing and Urban Development. Each day, he saw the struggles of single mothers living in projects without the help of the children's father.

Despite my best efforts, he still felt that this was going to be my future. And while he offered his support, he did not intend to save me from my actions. I had to understand the consequences.

It was in that moment that I realized that I could not rely on anyone else. Whether I liked it or not, I was going to have to put on my big-girl pants, accept my responsibility, and be an adult. I had two little people on the way who would be watching me, and I refused to let them down.

They deserved a fairy tale, of their own.

I laid out a game plan for myself, yet even with my game plan in hand, the move back to Connecticut proved to be more challenging than I anticipated. My initial goal was to find a job as a substitute teacher and work as long as I could; saving as much money as possible. Since I was 21, I still had the benefit of being covered by my parents' health insurance.

However, my initial doctor's appointment changed all of that.

After my first ultrasound and comparing my ultrasounds from Virginia, my doctor, Dr. Tracie Brennan, noticed that "Twin B" was not growing at the same rate as "Twin A" so she decided to err on the side of caution and put me on bedrest at the beginning of September!

My goal of working and saving money completely went out of the window. Still, my parents were amazing. They were going to help as much as they could and get me through bedrest. Lord knows I needed the help. The twins weren't due until January.

Plan B had to go into effect. I was convinced that after having the twins, I'd be able to easily find a teaching position. While my "job+benefits=financial freedom" plan had taken a detour, it was not totally off-course.

At this point, you may be wondering, "What about the father?" Let's just say he had not yet been fitted for his Knight-In-Shining-Armor gear, and whether I liked it or not, I was on my own.

However, that's for next week's sermon.

For ten weeks, I went back and forth to weekly doctor appointments, enduring steroid shots to help "Twin B" grow and countless tests and ultrasounds. Then, at a regularly scheduled ultrasound appointment, my team of doctors decided that "Twin B" was still not growing fast enough. They decided to schedule an emergency C-section for that afternoon.

The day was a complete blur. Then, at 9:42 and 9:45 pm, Mandell Clinton and Bryce Edward were born, 3 ½ lbs and 2 ½ lbs, eight weeks early. They were two, extremely healthy, tiny baby boys, and we quickly learned that Bryce, aka "Twin B," halted his own growth by completely wrapping himself up in the umbilical cord, head to toe, due to his constant in-utero acrobatics.

They were my tiny, already-funny, little men.

Since the twins were so small, they would have to stay in the hospital until they reached 5 lbs each. Considering they both

LOST a pound right after birth, it was going to be a long road home.

On my third day in the hospital, I was visited by the hospital accounts clerk. She wanted to know what insurance I had for the kids. "I'm covered by my father's insurance," I explained to her. "Well, yes, *you* are, but not the kids." Since the boys had to stay beyond the standard three days, my father's insurance would not cover them. There I was, a college-educated, unemployed, brand new single mother of two, with no income, and no way to pay for children's pending long-term hospital stay.

There went Plans C, D, *and* E!

The next day, the hospital social worker came to visit. Since I had a C-section, I had at least four to six weeks before I could consider working, and the boys had about six to ten weeks ahead of them. My only option was to sign up for Medicaid, W.I.C., and welfare. It seemed that my father's fears were coming true. My degree didn't matter. I was broke, living with my parents, and now I was a parent. I had a decision to make. I could let this break me or propel me.

That day in the hospital, after signing all of my welfare paperwork, I felt like a failure. My parents had done everything to make sure my life was perfect.

At that moment, I felt that I had destroyed everything. I mourned over the fairy tale; that perfect life. And then suddenly, I realized it was all a figment of my imagination.

The fairy tale that I was trying so hard to outrun wasn't a fairy tale at all. My parents fought like any other normal couple. My brother had some less than princely moments of defiance. My neighbors had just as many issues as we did. My friends and I dealt with racism on a regular basis.

And frankly, I was kind of a brat.

It was NEVER the fairy tale I thought it was. The truth was, my parents worked their tails off daily to give my brother and me everything that they could. It felt like a fairy tale because of the LOVE that we were shown every day. At that moment, I realized that I did not have to live up to some impossible goal.

I had to learn to love myself and show my children the same love that I had been shown.

That was the real fairy tale. That was the real *happily ever after*. And I was going to have it no matter what.

Once I realized that the fairy tale for myself and my children would be reclaimed through hard work and love, I began working on myself. I knew that there were things about Maya that had to change so that we could to have the life we deserved.

Here are the ten things I learned from my experience, in order to reclaim my happily ever after:

Maya Lynn's Happily Ever After Toolkit

1. *Know who you are and whose you are.* Remember when Jesse Jackson said, "I know I'm somebody because God don't make no junk?" That's your first tool. To reclaim your fairy tale, you must recognize that you are a child of God, and therefore, you are perfectly made to live the life He intended for you! I don't remember seeing anywhere in the Bible that I had to struggle every single day of my

life to go to heaven. You're intended to prosper and be a shining example of His goodness, grace, and mercy. The moment you accept this is the moment you will begin to walk in your purpose.

2. *Recognize that their opinions don't impact your reality.* You're going to have people who disagree with what you're doing. Especially the ones who claim to love you the most. Everybody who smiles in your face isn't your friend, so it is important to know that what you are trying to do in your life is for you. Other people's opinions are of no consequence. If you were walking in His purpose, that is the only opinion that matters.

3. *The devil didn't do it; you did.* When we make mistakes, it's very easy to blame other people. Nevertheless, you need to own up to your mess-ups! There isn't some grand puppeteer controlling your actions. Every decision you make is a decision that belongs to you. Once you own it, you can make the moves to fix it. However, you can't fix what you won't admit to.

4. *Pray. Then get up and work.* So, I am a church girl. I believe in the power of prayer. I believe that the Lord will answer my sincerest prayers to Him. "Faith without works is dead." God is not a magical genie, positioned to grant your every wish. You have to earn that blessing! It's there for you, but it will not be dropped in your lap.

Yes, pray for whatever it is that you want to happen in your life. Be still and listen to His direction. Then, get up and get to work.

5. *Laugh every chance you get. Especially in the mirror.* Now, look Sis, you have to stop taking yourself so seriously, okay? Have you been on social media lately? Everyone is so in love with themselves! You would think other people don't make mistakes. On the contrary, we all do! No one is perfect. Sometimes I mess up so badly on something that I just have to sit on the edge of my bed and laugh. We have to remember that God has a sense of humor (I mean, have you seen a platypus?) Stop being so critical of yourself. Realize that you're going to mess things up. Laugh it off, figure out how to fix it, and move on!

6. *Love everyone. Then leave them alone.* This is connected to tool # 2, not taking people's opinions as gospel. The ones who love you the most will always have a lot to say. Sometimes, the folks that you love the most will do the most damage. It is okay to love people from afar; that's what social media is for. Surround yourself with people who will support your dream and help you grow. Everyone can come to the book signing.

7. *Your job isn't enough. Financial stress can be overwhelming.* While we all probably were taught

the same lesson, go to school and find a good job with benefits, it is no longer sufficient. Get more income streams. Start a side business. Learn to invest. Buy some real estate. Whatever you do, start it now. You want to repair your roof when it is sunny because you can be an employee of the month today and on the unemployment line the next.

8. *Start somewhere. Right now.* We are constantly putting plans off. Waiting for the right moment. Next year. Next month. When our taxes come back. The only moment that we are promised is the one we are in right now. Waiting for the "perfect" time in an imperfect world is fruitless. Claim your moment and start working on your future now.

9. *Stop comparing yourself to other people.* No one can run your race for you. Every moment in your life has led you to where you are right now. So, don't look left and don't look right. Your future won't belong to anyone else but you.

And lastly...

10. *You have everything you need to win inside of your right now.* You are not a mistake. You are perfectly made. Every cell has been designed to handle every version of you. You just have to tap into yourself and

recognize that you were born to succeed. What you succeed in is up to you. Every excuse has been stripped away. You are naked, reborn. So reach inside yourself and awaken your greatness!

For so long, I thought that I would never rediscover the fairy tale my parents provided for me. I never realized that what I thought was an ideal life was simply the overpowering love they showed me in everything they did. My true happiness did not lie in attaining the "perfect" life; it was never perfect. Rather, my future depended on me learning to love myself, understanding that I had all I needed to succeed, and passing that love and determination on to my children. My fairy tale did not exist in some faraway land; it existed inside of me.

So, grab a mirror, Sista, and you'll see your happily ever after staring back at you!

Light and love!

Now You See Me, Now You Don't

VEDA GREEN

"Behind the cloud, the sun is still shining."
~ Abraham Lincoln

My bestie tagged me in a picture on Facebook.

When I saw the picture, I instantly began to laugh. Boy oh boy! It was probably around 1980 or '81, and my bestie and I were standing in front of the sign on the church lawn. She was wearing a red dress with a pattern that I cannot describe and a white cotton blouse underneath. One of her socks was drooping lower than the other, and she had a bang that, looking at its tightness, was without question set the night before on a pink sponge roller.

I stood next to her, wearing a white blouse, ironed crisply, and a red maxi skirt with flowers on it. My two thick ponytails were swollen from the Georgia heat, and my edges were fuzzy.

I don't know who coordinated my footwear, but I was sporting white open-toed sandals and white socks.

Truth be told, I probably served as my own stylist.

Looking at that picture brought back such sweet memories. My bestie and I were hugging tightly. My long, lanky arm was wrapped tightly around her neck, and she returned the love by wrapping her arm around my waist. And if you know anything about Black girls you already know where our other hands were... yep... on our hips!

We were young, innocent little girls who spent time jumping rope, playing with dolls and laughing about our little boy crushes.

My best friend and I were inseparable!

I tapped my phone, zoomed in on the picture, and took a closer look at my face. My smile was wide, and my eyes were bright. I was leaning in toward my bestie giving her all the excitement and energy that I had at that moment. I was so happy. The little girl in that picture was full of love, laughter, and life.

That was Veda! That was me!

When I look back on my childhood, I was so blessed! Although I grew up in Jennings Homes, a low-income housing development in Augusta, GA, I never knew I was 'low income.' I didn't know I was on welfare until I was a college graduate and married with kids! My older sister crushed my champagne dreams one day while we were talking on the phone. I was shocked! I know this sounds funny, but I was truly shocked. My mouth dropped opened and out of it came the words, "I ate government cheese?"

My sister hollered, "Yeah girl, and you LOVED it!"

We laughed until we cried!

You may be wondering why I didn't know I grew up on welfare. Here's why... my mother was proud!

SHEEEE didn't talk about the food stamps.

WEEEEE didn't talk about the food stamps.

NOBODY talked about the food stamps!

In fact, my sisters were sent to the store with our food stamps tucked into a wallet. They were told to pull out only what they needed, NOT the whole book. I was too young to go to the store alone, so I never got the wallet.

That's why I never knew!

A few days later, I looked at that photo again of my best friend and me. It made me wonder if I always had that much life and energy, so I went through some old photo albums of my days growing up. In nearly every picture, I was spunky and bright. I had the biggest smile and the most animated expressions.

There were quite a few pictures of me standing in front of our church congregation holding a microphone. I remember being quite the songbird. I read somewhere that my middle name, Lynette, means "songbird." I also read that it means "idol."

Put those two meanings together, and you know what you get? YES! I should've been on American Idol!

OK. Maybe not, but a girl can dream!

Anyway, I remember singing in church a lot! Every time I got the chance to sing, my song selection was "Pass It On." The first verse started with the words, *"It only takes a spark to get a fire going; and soon all those around will warm up to its glowing."*

I sang that song ALL THE TIME! I loved it! I sang it so much that my older sister called me Sparky! I never really thought much about the song or the nickname given to me as a joke, but now I see how that song and the name fit me to a T.

As a little girl, I was the spark that would start the fire of fun, excitement, laughter, and love! Sparky was that little girl whose glow was inviting and easy to warm up to! I had a big smile, a big heart, and an even bigger personality. I was loved and encouraged to be the best me I could be. The seeds of hope, ambition, and a winning spirit were planted and cultivated in my soul! I was Veda Lynette Hightower, and there was nothing I couldn't accomplish!

I always believed in myself, and I worked to achieve the greatest success. I was a spark, and my glow rivaled the sun's brightness!

You may be thinking, "Wow! Veda, you were so cocky and full of yourself!" And I'll say unashamedly that you're right! I was!

I think ALL children should be cocky and full of themselves in the most positive way. I didn't know what it meant to have low self-esteem or hide my shine. I was bright from birth, and everyone who loved me fanned my flames!

When I was almost 14, I took my shine and went to live with my older sister in Virginia. My mother wanted me to experience a different level of education that I couldn't get at the public high school I was zoned to attend in Augusta. I'd attended Christian school through 8th grade, but she couldn't afford to send me away to the Christian boarding academy, so she decided to let me move "up north."

The summer of 1984 was the last one I spent in GA. This southern (not country) girl relocated to Alexandria, VA.

I left the home, the church, *and* the school where I'd been raised, to embark on a new adventure. I had no idea what was waiting for me there. What I did know is that I was with my big sister and I didn't have to go to high school "down south."

As we drove the 10 hours from Augusta to Alexandria, I can remember being excitedly scared. I was excited about the newness of living in another state and going to a new school, but as nervously afraid for the same reason.

When I arrived in Alexandria to attend Thomas A. Edison High School, I couldn't register for any classes. My sister didn't realize that my mom had to give her legal custody to enroll me in school, so I had to wait on the guardianship papers to be approved and accepted by the school district. When everything was finalized, I was able to enroll, but I was two weeks behind.

I soon found out that coming from "down south" put me farther behind than that! I was a full year behind my Virginia peers academically! I sat in Algebra class looking like Madea saying, "I don't know nothing 'bout this Al Jarreau" because I hadn't taken pre-Algebra in 8th grade. I had NO idea WHAT that lady at the blackboard was talking about.

It wasn't until I understood that the letters represented numbers that I caught on to Al Jarreau!

My Algebra grade jumped from a C- to a B+ by the end of the year. By the end of my 10th-grade year, I was nearly a straight "A" student.

That stupid B in Geometry messed me up!

The summer before my Junior year, I moved to MD, and that's when I met him.

I was 15.

He was cute, a little older, and all the girls liked him. They had known him for years, but I was the new girl in town, and they assured me that he wouldn't like me because he didn't like any of them. What did they mean, he wouldn't like me? I'm Veda! They bet me he wouldn't, and I bet them he would! Having the winning attitude that I did, I took my new friends up on their challenge.

By the time I turned 16, the age of official dating, he was my boyfriend. I'd gotten the guy that every girl wanted but was too afraid to go after. Not this girl! I went after what I wanted, and I got it! That was the Veda I'd always been! If you told me I couldn't, shouldn't or wouldn't, I'd prove you wrong every time. I was a winner! I got the guy! I was shining even brighter now! *I was so excited, and I just couldn't hide it.* I didn't want to either!

Sadly, however, my light would soon be diminished.

It began to happen when I was 16 going on 17. We'd been dating for almost a year when he dropped a bomb on me that would shake the foundation of who I was at my core.

One evening after choir rehearsal, while driving me home, he told me something that would be the first of many solar eclipsing experiences with him. We were sitting in the driveway when I mentioned the song the choir was going to sing at church the next day. "I love that song!" I beamed and began singing the solo part.

He cut me off mid-performance and said, "You know, you're not really a strong soloist. You have more of a choir voice."

I stared at him blankly. I didn't know how to respond. I wanted to cry, but instead, I swallowed the lump in my throat and asked, "What's a choir voice?"

He said, "You know. You have a voice that sounds better in a choir, not singing a solo."

Oh wow! THE SHADE!!!

It suddenly got cold in the car! My shine had been sucked into a black hole! I looked at him, then past him out the driver side window. I couldn't make eye contact. My feelings were hurt, but I smiled to hide the pain. Did he say I had a choir voice? Yes, that's what he said. What's wrong with that?

It's not what he said, but what I heard. I heard my boyfriend say, "You're not good enough. You don't deserve to be up front as the soloist. Your place is in the background."

I should've said something to him to let him know that I WAS good enough, but I remained silent because I wanted his love.

Everybody loved me, and I wanted him to love me too.

So, to keep his affection, I simply tucked my voice away and trusted that he was right. After all, he was the musician. He came from a family of singers. He knew what he was talking about.

At that point, sitting in his Ford Escort, I believed that he was right, so I exchanged my shine for his love and acceptance. That night, I allowed his words to put an instant muzzle, not only on my vocal cords, but also on my voice!

Seven years after I found out I had a choir voice, I married him. I was 23 years old and much too young to jump the broom, but it was the next "right" thing to do. I'd graduated from college, secured a job and moved out of my mother's house.

What else was there to do?

So, after living on my own for less than six months, I got married! I mean, I HAD to get married! I was paying bills, cooking meals and wearing heels! Yep, heels, in the boardroom AND the bedroom! I was doing all the things a wife should do, but I wasn't a wife yet. I was a Christian who was living wrong and on my way to hell! I had to make everything right in the eyes of the Lord because Paul said in 1 Corinthians 7:9, *"It's better to marry than to burn!"* and Lord knows I didn't want to burn!

I got married so I wouldn't burn! Yeah, I know. I found out later that's NOT what that scripture meant. LOL!

Anyway... on May 20, 1994, I became a Mrs. I was overjoyed and elated! I felt like a weight had been lifted off my chest and I was back in God's favor! Hallelujah! I spent the first years of our marriage as a happy and doting wife. My husband was everything to me! I was thrilled that I had found the one!

Everybody who knew us said I'd hooked the best fish in the sea and honestly, I felt the same way. I was so blessed to have him as my husband. I loved every aspect of this man from his curly hair to his bow legs. I was thankful that he loved God and that he took care of his responsibilities.

Because I'd grown up without my father, I always knew I wanted to have a "til death do us part" marriage.

No divorce! EVER!

I did everything possible to make sure my husband didn't leave me like my father had. When we had children, I became even more focused on being a good wife and mother because I'd never experienced a man being anything but absent. I was determined that my children would never, ever go through that.

At this point in my life, as a mother, I didn't realize that my shine was being hidden. It really didn't matter much. Life was all about the kids anyway. If I had to sacrifice my shine for the sake of my children, I would, and I did. I refused to ever let them experience the life that I had without a father.

While I had a good childhood, surrounded by love, I was never Daddy's little girl. I never had *that* kind of love, and I'd be damned if my daughter was going to end up like me. Somebody was going to be a Daddy's girl! If it couldn't be me, surely it would be her! So, I swallowed my emotions. I didn't speak up for myself.

I didn't do the things that made me happy. I stuck to the script and played my role very well. I didn't do anything that would rock the boat. I endured internal storms to maintain external peace. I did that for years, but the kids began to grow up, and that shit got old! I got tired of being unhappy and depressed! I got tired of being overlooked and not considered! I got tired of holding my tongue, not saying what I needed to say and getting what I needed to have! I got sick and tired of being sick and tired, so I went to therapy, dealt with those father issues and grew the hell up!

When I did that, I felt free! I knew it was time to make some changes and do the things that brought me happiness! I wanted to live! I wanted to be the woman that God created me to be, and I wanted to be that woman with my husband! But that's not what happened! It didn't go the way I'd seen it in my head.

In my head, it went like this: "Babe, I've been going to therapy to deal with my father issues. It was hard, but I did it! Now that I have worked through that junk, I want us to be partners in this marriage. I want us to work together, grow together, and be in this thang together!" I honestly believed that my husband would hear me, rejoice that I'd made such great progress with my issues, and escort me to my rightful place in our marriage, but I was wrong.

What I'd conjured up in my mind didn't play out that way at all in real life! My husband didn't change. He remained the same responsible, hardworking, churchgoing guy he'd always been. He didn't see the need to do anything differently. He was just fine with life and made no apologies for being who he was.

In his eyes, there was nothing wrong, so he didn't feel any great need to adjust his behavior. He loved me by taking care of his family, and he felt that was a good enough expression of his love. When I told him I needed more, he couldn't understand how I could need any more than what he was already giving.

When I shared with him that I didn't feel like I was first in his life, that he made other people a priority over me, he told me that didn't make sense to him. When I expressed that I felt invisible and unimportant, he simply said, "I'm sorry you feel that way," and kept on with his regularly scheduled program of work, church, kids, ministry, etc.

When I told him that I was unhappy in our marriage, he stood in our living room and told me to go and find my happiness.

After all of that, I still couldn't accept the fact that he wasn't going to change. I just couldn't let go of my *"til death do us part"* dream! So, I kept talking to him.

I kept trying to get him to see me! I wanted him to love me in the way that I needed to be loved. I explained to him how empty I was and how I felt like I was dying inside. I'd dealt with my "daddy issues" and was no longer grieving over the loss of my father's affection, but the wounds inflicted by my dad were healing and still present. They had scabs covering them, and every time my husband looked past me and continued to ignore my requests, he would knock the scabs off, and I'd bleed afresh!

The pain was deep, and I hurt so badly. I didn't know how much more I could take. I fell into deep depression again.

Why couldn't he see me?

Ironically, my turning point came on May 20, 2016, twenty-two years after I said I do! I realized that my husband was not seeing me didn't make me invisible. I was invisible because I allowed myself to be hidden behind his cloud for so many years!

I'd dimmed my shine because I was afraid that I would outshine him. I'd become the submissive wife that Paul talks about in Ephesians 5:22-24. Yeah, another misinterpreted scripture. I submitted to his life plan, his dreams, and what he wanted. I had not lived my dreams. I had not kept my promises to myself. I hadn't made myself a priority!

How could I expect him to put me first when I hadn't put myself first! Here I was approaching 50, and I was wasting time trying to get HIM to see me when I wasn't even seeing me! What a reality punch in the gut!

OUCH!!!

But that's not the only gut punch I got! Reality hit me again! What about my children? How was hiding my shine affecting them? They'd watched me hide behind the clouds of fear, silence, and discontent for years. They saw me come home every day from a job that I hated when I really wanted to pursue my dream of Building Brighter Kids. How would they learn to live their dreams if I didn't live mine?

What's worse is my daughter watched me swallow my emotions when I should've spoken up for myself! I'd taught her to suppress her feelings by failing to open my mouth and saying what I needed to say! Hiding impacted my older son too! I was showing him what kind of wife to choose for himself! I was telling him that it was OK to have a wife who was timid and afraid to express her feelings. I don't know right now how I've impacted my youngest, but I know I was shortchanging all my kids by unplugging my shine and giving away my power! I'd squeezed the lively, bright-eyed, optimistic dreamer into a box and closed the lid!

I had hidden my true self so that I wouldn't shine too brightly. But all of that is over! I may have a choir voice, but I will never be silenced again!

It no longer matters if my husband changes or not. His behavior doesn't dictate my happiness, and it will not block my shine. Because I've learned to embrace the profound statement, "It is what it is!" I've decided to live a life that will bring me joy.

Doing so will allow me to spend my remaining days on this earth shining brightly! And that's what I want for you!

Don't hide your shine any longer! If you know it's time for you to shine again, here are some tips that can help you get your shine back.

- **IDENTIFY YOUR CLOUDS!** Determine who or what is blocking your shine and deal with it. Be honest with yourself. Don't make excuses any longer!

- **OWN YOUR SHINE!** You must know who you are and what your shine is! Your shine is innately you, and it illuminates when you do the things that bring you joy! Do the thing that you've been hiding behind the cloud! More than likely that thing is connected to your purpose!

- **ALLOW IT TO RAIN!** Clouds sometimes bring showers, but it's OK to let yourself cry and feel the pain that comes from being behind a cloud. Crying is good for the soul. Just don't stay in that storm cloud. Let the sun come out again.

- **YOU MUST KNOW WHAT BRINGS THE SUN OUT!** What makes you shine? Is it music or dancing? Is it baking or painting? I found the thing that brings back shine is always connected to some form of creativity!

- **CONNECT WITH YOUR WIND!** My sister is my wind! She blows my clouds away! How? She reminds me of my shine! Find somebody who will blow your clouds away and remind you of your shine!

- **AFFIRM YOUR SHINE!** I affirm my shine by reciting *"Our Deepest Fear"* by Marianne Anderson or "Phenomenal Woman" by Maya Angelou! Stand in the mirror and affirm yourself! Speak positively about your shine!

- **SHINE ABOVE THE CLOUDS!** Sometimes we don't have control over the clouds in our lives. Shine anyway! Even when the clouds block its rays, the sun is still shining brightly above them!

- **SHINE FOR YOUR CHILDREN!** Just like the moon needs the sun to shine, your kids need you to shine so they can shine too! Even though we don't see the sun at night, it's still shining because we see the moon. The same is true for our children. They will reflect our light even when we are no longer with them.

Now that you've decided to shine, nothing can stop you! Even with clouds all around, remember that you were created to shine!

So, shine on!

... and never be invisible again!

About the Authors

Audra R. Upchurch

Audra is passionate about helping women with clear vision produce elite, high-level book collaborations that elevate their brand and provide a unique, educational, and profitable experience to the lead author and contributors. She understands that owning and sharing our individual stories is an important ingredient if we are ever to leave a lasting legacy for those that follow.

Born and raised in Brooklyn, New York, to a mother who suffers with mental illness, Audra lived in a household that was extremely unstable. As a result, she was homeless by the age of fifteen, a single mother at seventeen, and quickly heading down a dark path; however, through prayer and the belief that she deserved more, Audra persevered, graduated college, earned her MBA, and has been able to live her best life. Today, she is not only married to an amazingly wonderful man; together they have six adult children and four beautiful grandchildren.

As a 3x bestselling author, speaker, and entrepreneur, Audra helps women find their voice, shape their stories, and navigate the writing process to deliver a meaningful manuscript.

She and her husband are the CEO and CIO, respectively, of **The UPFAM Group, LLC**, an organization that captures our philanthropic, mentorship, and community-based activities.

She gives her heart, time, and treasure to supporting programs that help women, families, and youth struggling with mental health issues and homelessness; including the Hampton Roads affiliate of *Stand Up For Kids*. Audra believes that life is all about choices, and she thanks you for choosing to connect with her!

Feel free to email her at info@audraupchurch.com and engage with her on all social media outlets at @AuthenticAudra

Ann M. Dillard

Ann Dillard is a licensed marriage and family therapist, speaker, educational trainer and consultant, and a global change agent. She served as a school-based mental health therapist before establishing her private practice. In her practice, Ann uses her exceptional ability to connect with teens as a tool to provide strategies and life skills that transform their minds and lives.

During her teenage years, Ann was plagued with sexual and physical abuse that contributed to issues with low self-esteem, abandonment, suicidal ideations and compulsive overeating. As an immigrant to the United States, Ann uses a unique combination of her life stories and experiences that chronical her journey of learning and unlearning culture. Her strength as a connector inspires and motivates her audiences across very diverse milieus.

As a co-author in the anthology Unchain My Legacy, and as the owner of KIP Consulting Services and host of the weekly Facebook LIVE show TEEN Talk LIVE, Ann addresses real issues that teens are faced with in today's society.

Ann is also the founder of the non-profit organization Project Safety Nets, whose mission is to create sustainable living in developing communities through education, health, and economic development.

Ann and her husband Joseph, have been married for twenty-nine years and have four successful adult children and three beautiful grandchildren. To learn more about her work, contact her at:

Email: Kipconsult@msn.com
Website: www.anndillard.com
Facebook: https://www.facebook.com/AnnDillard.MA.LMFT

Janika N. Joyner

Janika N. Joyner is a wife and mother of two sons. She earned her Master of Social Work with a Clinical Concentration from Norfolk State University in Norfolk, VA.

Janika is a Licensed Clinical Social Worker in Virginia who specializes in trauma with a certification as a clinical trauma professional through the International Association of Trauma Professionals (IATP).

She is a member of the National Association of Social Workers (NASW) and Black Therapists Rock (BTR). She has over ten years of experience working with children and adolescents in the residential setting. While helping her clients heal Janika began working on her own personal development which led her to begin addressing her adverse childhood experiences.

She founded Elevation Counseling Services, LLC to address the effects that adverse childhood experiences have on the mind, body, and spirit. Janika is the author of three journals:

"Owning It: My Parent is an Addict," "Owning It: Changing my Distorted Thinking," and "Adjust Your Crown Black Girls."

Janika is committed to serving the community and her clients as she helps them heal through writing their trauma narratives and owning their stories.

"In order to heal, we must be REAL"- Janika N. Joyner

For more information, visit: elevationcounselingservice.com

Illiona Illy Okereke

Illiona Okereke, also known as Illy, is a certified school counselor and licensed associate counselor. Hailing from East Orange, NJ, Illy received her bachelor's in Psychology at The College of New Jersey (TCNJ). After completing her master's in Counseling Services from Rider University, she returned to TCNJ and earned an educational specialist (a post Master's degree) in Marriage and Family Therapy. She has over ten years of experience working in nonprofit, school, and community settings. She also serves in leadership at her church.

Fluent in Haitian Creole, Illy has offered academic and emotional support to many students (K-12) and their families transitioning to the U.S. after the earthquake in Haiti. She is passionate about helping families of underserved populations navigate the school system, foster cultural pride, and receive mental health services. In 2016, Illy was honored with TCNJ's Social Justice and Advocacy Award.

Illy's professional and personal experiences have shaped her mission to assist caregivers and helping professionals to optimize their ability in serving others by caring for their own mental health. As a result, she founded MESH with Illy, a platform in which she promotes mental, emotional, and spiritual health (MESH) through blogging and speaking through various outlets.

To connect with Illiona Okereke, visit www.meshwithilly.com or email info@meshwithilly.com.

Sabra Starnes

Sabra and her twin were adopted as infants in a closed adoption. Growing up in a transracial family in the Midwest had many joys and challenges. Sabra and her family experienced racism and discrimination as a transracial family. Sabra learned to persevere and be a strong advocate for herself. And at a young age, she knew she wanted to help others.

She provides adoption counseling using attachment-based therapies connected with expressive therapies. She facilitates a monthly foster and adoptive support group, and Love and Logic parenting workshops. As an expert adoption therapist for the past 20 years, she has the personal experience and professional training to work with families who have been touched by adoption and foster care. She is a strong advocate for children who are in care to have permanency or reunify with their birth families.

Sabra has a Masters in Social Work from Catholic University and Masters in Education from American University. She has her certification in Life Crisis Skills, Sand tray, Play Therapy, Trauma, Loss, and Grief. She is a Parenting the love and logic Way. She specializes in adoption, foster care, parenting issues, and skills.

Sabra is married to the love of her life Krushae; sons Larry and Rasheed, and a ten-month-old granddaughter, Alayna.

E: sabrastarnes@gmail.com
W: sabrastarnes.com

Michele Mikki Jones

Michele Mikki Jones is an executive assistant, author, and speaker. A graduate of Tidewater Community College with an Associates in Applied Science in Human Services, she is also a current student at Norfolk State University pursuing a Bachelor's Degree in Social Work and founder of Being My Sista's Keeper and Living with Lupus 365. Michele's ability to survive for the past eighteen years with Lupus enables her to encourage, support and inspire others who have been diagnosed, to understand and thrive with such a debilitating disease.

Michele is the author of The Poetry of My Life and Lupus 365-A Journey Thru Life (The Journal) and is currently finishing her second book of poetry – Gathering the Pieces. As a survivor and motivational speaker and advocate for Lupus, Michele offers a wide range of personal experience and tips that focus on living healthy and self-care. She also sponsors a team with the Lupus Foundation of America – Lupus Loop! – Alice's Garden and is a team member with Keep It Movin'- Kim. Michele is an avid runner and has completed 5 Half Marathons and numerous 10K, 8K and 5K races.

Michele has four adult children and nine grandchildren.

Learn more about Michele and the work she does at www. sistaskeeper.com.

Tearanie Wilson-Parker

Tearanie Parker is a Financial Professional, Amazon Best Selling Author, and Speaker. A graduate of Regent University with a Masters in Education. She also holds three Securities Licenses, and is the founder of "Funding An Empire."

Tearanie's diverse background, and her ability to be candid regarding her own financial mistakes has enabled her to have a relational approach that inspires others to regain control, expand, or completely change their financial destiny. Tearanie is the author of "Funding An Empire, What My Parents Didn't Teach Me About Money." And the co-author of "Lemon-Aid Chronicles" and Amazon's best-seller, "Unchain Me Mama."

A motivational and financial speaker, she also hosts a radio segment called "Funding An Empire," offering a broad range of financial tips that focus on practical, real-life financial issues.

Contact Tearanie at www.fundinganempire.com

Tonya Renada Moore

Tonya Renada Moore was born in the back seat of her uncle's red Opel (German car) in the parking lot of DC General Hospital in Washington DC.

She was delivered by her grandmother, and her middle name, Renada, was chosen by her uncle and oddly enough means "reborn."

Tonya was raised in the District of Columbia for the first thirteen years of her life and later moved to the suburbs of Maryland where she graduated high school in Bladensburg, MD. At age 28, she and her son moved to the Hampton Roads area to further her career with the U.S. Army Corps of Engineers, Norfolk district.

She earned a bachelor's degree from the University of Phoenix in Phoenix AZ. Her vast accounting knowledge and experiences span over two decades. She is currently employed by Portsmouth Redevelopment and Housing Authority in Portsmouth VA as a financial specialist. She is a board member on her neighborhood civic league and a leader in her church. Tonya now realizes her options for her future are limitless.

Tonya is married to Carlos Moore and has two children, Jacoby and Jasmine, and currently resides in Chesapeake, Virginia with her husband and her mom.

She can be contacted through Facebook, Tonya R Moore, IG, mooretonyar, email tonya.moore757@gmail.com

Patrice Trice Brown

Patrice R. Brown is a bestselling author in the anthology Unchain Me Mama which was released in 2017. Unchain Me Mama hit number one on Amazon's bestsellers list in 2017. Now, in this anthology Unchain My Legacy, Patrice will be a two-time bestselling author.

Patrice is a retired police officer and US Navy Veteran. Patrice is also the former owner and president of a private security firm located in Brooklyn, New York. Patrice earned her associate's degree in police sciences from John Jay College and has plans to return to school for her Bachelor's in police sciences.

Patrice has always had a knack for making others smile or laugh even when they didn't want to. She protects those she loves from the harsh realities they experience in their lives with laughter, advice, and support in any way she can. She is a woman of her word. When you're around her, you are in a 'no judgment zone.' She loves to entertain. If you're in her close-knit circle of Sis-Stars, you have a friend for life.

To connect, email her at thrivingpatrice@gmail.com

Davina Jennile

Davina Jennile is a Behaviorist, Relationologist Coach, Speaker, and Early Interventionist Clinical Trainer that gives a fresh raw and real perspective on mental illness, career development, autism, entrepreneurship, and relationship coaching for single and divorced women. She is a graduate of Ball State University with a Master of Art in Applied Behavior Analysis, with a specialization in Autism and Neuropsychology. Davina received her undergraduate degree from Georgia Southern University. Davina currently works as a private practice contractor to other companies and the state as a behaviorist and trainer.

Davina's combined her professional and personal experience of understanding "learned behaviors" and started Davina Jennile, LLC. She uses her passion and background to help other single and divorced women with finding the answers to "Am I ready for a relationship now? Have I self-healed and can I move forward? What does a healthy relationship look like for me?" and women entrepreneurship by understanding how our "brain function" of fear can play a psychological obstacle on entrepreneurship and overcoming our fears to successfully reach our goals.

Outside of work, Davina is actively volunteering within her community, working out, or with her two beautiful cats. She is an active member of the Junior League of Atlanta (JLA) and Black Therapist Rock (BTR). To connect with her, email at info@ davinajennile.com or visit www.davinajennile.com

Sandra De Greene

This is Sandra's second anthology; the first being Unchain Me Mama which became a number one bestseller in the year it was released.

Sandra was born, raised and is currently living in Brooklyn, NY. She is a former member of the US Army and currently serving in the Army National Guard. She recently completed a tour in Afghanistan. She is a single mom of a special needs adult. She has an Associates in Accounting and a Bachelors in Business Administration with a concentration in Accounting. She is currently the Office Manager and the lone female working for a privately-owned Construction Company in Brooklyn, NY.

Sandra believes that everyone has a talent or gift, but for many reasons, people choose not to pursue their passion. From childhood, Sandra created stories and played them out in her mind. As an adult, she held the dream of being a writer. Thanks to the visionary author for this book, Audra R. Upchurch, she now has a launching pad to catapult her dream to fulfillment. She hopes to one day write faith-based books based on real life. She hopes to inspire others to pursue their own dreams.

To connect with Sandra email her at greene-s1@msn.com

Maya Lynn

From training award-winning educators and developing life-long learners to helping women unlock their true talents, Maya Harris is driven to make education and self-growth a priority in all households.

As an educational advocate and trainer, Maya works with public schools, private schools, and nonprofits to train students using strategies that focus on the learner, not the test. Maya's methods not only have helped students pass state assessments for the first time, but also help build confidence in students that allow them to enjoy learning again.

Maya is the founder of LAMA Learning, an educational service company that connects families to the best and brightest educators that are trained to work with students in a 1-to-1 setting to provide focused, quality instruction.

She is the author of What's Your Oil? Unmasking Your Hidden Talents, where she takes the reader through the story of the Widow's Oil (II Kings 4:1-7), how the widow helped Maya discover her entrepreneurial gifts and ways for YOU to begin your journey toward finding your true purpose.

Maya is also the founder of RVA Sistas United, an online, social organization based in Richmond, Virginia. RVA Sistas United is a community of women who have come together to bring about POSITIVE change in the Greater Richmond and Tri-Cities areas. Maya has dedicated her life to helping women unlock their passion and connect with other women, building a council of success.

Maya has two wonderful sons, Mandell and Bryce, and currently resides in Richmond, Virginia.

To connect with Maya, visit: www.mayalynn.co

Veda H. Green

Veda H. Green is a passionate teacher, gifted author, and dynamic speaker. A graduate of Old Dominion University with a Master's in Education, she is a veteran teacher with nearly 20 years of experience and the founder of Building Brighter Kids.

Veda's experience as a teacher and mother, coupled with her humorous storytelling skills, have enabled her to inspire women to embrace their past, heal from the wounds of that past, and create a brighter future for themselves and their children.

Veda is the author of Building Brighter Kids from Kindergarten to College and is currently writing the second book of the BBK book series. As a motivational speaker and educational trainer for schools, churches, parent organizations, and women's conferences, Veda offers her audience real-life tools, tips, and strategies to encourage them to step out of the darkness of their own past and to shine their light brightly!

Veda has been blessed with the privilege of mothering three beautiful children, and because of them, she has had the courage to live life unapologetically! Veda's motto is, "Live Fully. Laugh Loudly. Love Deeply." When Veda's not busy fulfilling her Building Brighter Kids dream or teaching science, she enjoys reading, dancing, and traveling.

You can connect with Veda at www.buildingbrighterkids.com or email her at buildingbrighterkids@gmail.com.